BIG BOOK OF CHRISTMAS KNITS

JORID LINVIK

Jorid's

BIG BOOK OF CHRISTMAS KNITS

OVER 70 SCANDINAVIAN HOLIDAY PATTERNS

Trafalgar **S**quare
North Pomfret, Vermont

First published in the United States of America in 2019 by
Trafalgar Square Books
North Pomfret, Vermont 05053

Originally published in Norwegian as *Jorids Julestrikk*.

Copyright © 2018 Jorid Linvik and Vega Forlag AS
English translation © 2019 Trafalgar Square Books

ISBN: 978-1-57076-952-8

Library of Congress Control Number: 2019905358

Interior design and layout: Johanne Hjorthol
Photography: Marthe Mølstre
Translation into English: Carol Huebscher Rhoades

Extra Materials: Visit joridweb.com/julestrikk

Printed in China

10 9 8 7 6 5 4 3 2 1

CONTENTS

PREFACE

I'm certainly not the only one who thinks Advent and the Christmas holidays are the best time of the year! The good feelings arrive on December 1 when the Advent stars and Advent candles are placed in my cottage window to mark the time leading up to Christmas.

December days go by quickly with all sorts of Christmas preparations—and Christmas interruptions! Christmas concerts and events eat up time in all the best ways, and at home there's plenty to keep you busy, too: presents to wrap, Christmas cakes and other tasty Christmas food to be prepared, and of course decorating the house so it's ready for Christmas. Sometimes it can be hard to hang on to your Christmas cheer in the face of it all.

We want to get the most out of Christmas, which means all these preparations can lead to stress instead of comfort. So don't forget to rest between activities! And what better way to take a break than sitting down for a few minutes to knit? You can ease your mind and relax, and make more gifts and decorations at the same time—a win-win situation. Perhaps you'll also be able to watch some TV or listen to music while you knit? Triple joy.

Besides, what's stopping you from starting early, if you're that type of person? Christmas gifts and decorations can be knitted all year long, so you'll have plenty of time to enjoy it.

This book was written precisely for those of you who want to give yourselves a reason to indulge in plenty of Christmas spirit. You'll find many knitting projects here that offer both comfort and utility, in big ways and small. All the projects in this book were designed with Christmas in mind, whether as gifts or toys and decorations.

Have a good Christmas!
Jorid Linvik
BODØ, NORWAY

BASICS FOR KNITTING THE PATTERNS IN THIS BOOK

If you're familiar with all the basic knitting techniques, there's nothing to stop you from knitting all the projects in this book. However, some of the projects will be easier than others. Many of the projects are suitable for beginners, while others will be a challenge without a bit more experience. Read through the entire pattern before you start to knit and make sure you understand how the project should be worked. In this introduction, you'll find explanations of the concepts in the book, charts, and the symbols used in them.

KNITTING BACK AND FORTH

Many of the projects are worked back and forth. In that case, you can work with two straight knitting needles or a circular. Always slip the first stitch on each row when knitting back and forth to make a smooth and neat edge. Edge stitches are not marked as such on the charts.

KNITTING IN THE ROUND

A number of the projects are worked in the round. Hats and larger items can be worked on a circular needle. You'll cast on all the stitches onto the circular, join them into a ring, and then knit around. If you want to knit something that has too few stitches to stretch all the way around a circular needle, you can use a set of 5 double-pointed needles. Cast on the required number of stitches, divide the stitches as evenly as possible onto 4 double-pointed needles, and join into a ring. Make sure the cast-on row isn't twisted so you won't have a twist in the piece. Use the fifth needle to knit with.

ROWS AND ROUNDS

A *row* is worked over all the stitches across a needle. A *round* includes all the stitches around in circular knitting.

GARTER RIDGE

Two rows of knitting back and forth make a garter ridge. To make a ridge in the round, knit 1 round and then purl 1 round (the purl round makes a ridge on the right side).

WORKING TWO-COLOR STRANDED PATTERNS

For some of the designs, you'll knit patterns in the round with two colors at the same time. When knitting the stitches, make sure both color strands stay on the wrong side throughout. Keep an eye on the strands ("floats") on the wrong side to make sure they aren't getting tight or pulling in.

DOMINANT COLOR

Most patterns with two colors have a prominent motif against a background—for example, the Advent calendar bags with the pattern figure motifs. For the smoothest possible result and so the motif can be clearly seen, it's important that you hold the yarn strand for the color used to work the motif below the yarn strand for the color used to work the background; hold them this way at the back of the work throughout.

If you knit with one color in each hand, the motif color should be worked by holding it in the left hand. If you hold both strands over the left index finger, the motif color should be held innermost on the finger (that is, below the fingernail and closer to you). The two strands should always be held the same way in relation to each other. If you change the position of the yarns, your work will be uneven.

KNITTING A THUMB OPENING

Mittens are easy to knit—at least up until the thumb. You begin at the lower edge of the mitten and work up to the thumbhole. The placement of the thumbhole is marked by a horizontal line on the chart.

The stitches directly above the line should be worked with scrap yarn, the "thumb strand." Use a smooth, contrast-color scrap yarn (preferably cotton) that will be easy to see.

Work in pattern up to (but not including) the first stitch above the heavy line. With the scrap yarn, knit the stitches above the heavy line—on the chart shown here, there are 11 of them. Slip the scrap yarn stitches back to the left needle and push both ends of the scrap yarn to the wrong side. Work in charted pattern over the scrap yarn stitches and then continue around in pattern.

When you later remove the scrap yarn, you'll have an opening so you can knit the thumb in the round. To remove scrap yarn, insert a double-pointed needle through the stitches below the scrap yarn and another double-pointed needle in the row above the scrap yarn. That way, you shouldn't lose any stitches. Carefully pick out the scrap yarn.

Begin knitting the thumb on the front of the thumb. On the first round of the thumb, you'll usually increase with 1 or 2 stitches picked up and knitted on either side of the thumb. At the beginning of the round (or, for example, on right side of a thumb gusset), knit into the stitch below the first stitch on needle (RLI—right-lifted increase); at the end (or, for example, on left side of thumb gusset), knit into the stitch below the previous stitch (LLI—left-lifted increase). The first row of the back of the thumb is worked with the stitches that really are "upside down". Work each of these stitches through the back loop for a smooth transition.

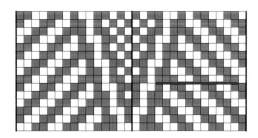

When the thumb is finished, you might see a little hole where the thumb began. Tighten any holes on the back of the work at the same time as you weave in the ends.

KNITTING A HEEL

Socks are also easy to knit, especially once you've worked the heel. This book has patterns for several pairs of socks and Christmas stockings, with various types of heel. The shaping for each type of heel is carefully explained. Some heels are worked back and forth with a heel flap and then decreased at the sides (the heel turn shaping), while others are worked around an opening made exactly as for the thumbhole opening in the previous section.

SEAMING WITH KITCHENER STITCH

To make a neat seam at the top of a sock or mitten, use Kitchener stitch. The result is smooth and more rounded than drawing the end of the yarn through the remaining stitches and tightening it. Kitchener stitch is also used to seam shoulders.

APPLIQUE OR DUPLICATE STITCH

At several points in various patterns, you'll be instructed to use duplicate stitch or applique over a few stitches so the motif will look as it should. This is so much fun to do—and the results will be eye-catching.

In some instances, it's worth "splitting" the yarn you are appliqueing with so the appliqued areas won't turn out thick or bulky; sew with only two of the plies of the yarn for a lighter result. On the other hand, it can work well to allow areas with duplicate stitch to stick out a little from the background. You can decide which you prefer—and you can always change your mind.

You can also use this technique if you want to embroider initials in the work or "write" something else. Or, if you made an error in the motif pattern, you can correct it with a few duplicate stitches.

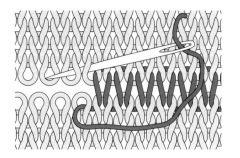

READING THE CHARTS

A) An encircled number on the chart refers back to the same number in the pattern instructions. The arrows between numbers indicate the rows/rounds described in the written text.

B) Heavy, vertical lines below the chart mark off the stitches on each needle. This makes it easier to see where you are in the pattern.

C) The numbers between the vertical lines tell you how many stitches are on that needle.

D) The number to the left of the chart gives the total number of stitches on the round/row.

E) A "notch" at the side of the pattern: When decreasing, there are fewer and fewer stitches on the needles and the pattern gets narrower. A "notch" also appears on the chart when there are a series of increases.

F) Dotted lines appear over the stitches which have been removed in the decreases. There are no stitches here. In some of the patterns, the dotted lines appear over stitches where there will later be increases.

SYMBOL KEYS FOR THE CHARTS

Every square on a chart corresponds to a stitch. Work the stitch with the color of the square. The symbols inside the squares indicate which stitch to use.

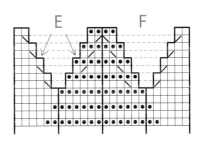

NOTE: Some chart symbols used are specific to this book, so always check the text against the chart to make sure you are working correctly.

Knit stitch (k): Knit on the right side (RS) of the work and knit on the wrong side (WS).

Purl stitch (p): Purl on the RS and purl on the WS.

Increase/make 1 (M1): Increase with the method which looks best for the patterning. A good method is to make 1: lift the strand between two stitches and knit into the back of the strand to twist it, or work right- and left-lifted increases (see below for specifics).

Yarnover (yo): Bring the yarn around the right needle once; on the next round, work as for the stitch indicated.

Right-Lifted Increase (RLI): Lift the top of the stitch below the next stitch and knit into it.

Left-Lifted Increase (LLI): Lift the top of the stitch below the previous stitch and knit into it.

Right-Leaning Decrease (k2tog): Knit two stitches together in the color indicated.

Left-Leaning Decrease (twisted decrease): There are several options:
K2tog tbl: Knit two stitches together through back loops = insert the needle through the 2 stitches from right to left along the row and knit them together.
Ssk: (sl 1 knitwise) 2 times; slide sts back onto left needle and knit the stitches together through back loops.
Sl 1, k1, psso: Sl 1 st knitwise, k1, pass slipped st over.
Join 3 stitches (sk2p): Slip the first stitch, knit the next 2 stitches together and pass the slipped stitch over.

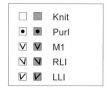

ABBREVIATIONS

BO	bind off (British = cast off)	M1	make = lift strand between 2 sts and knit into back loop		decreased
ch	chain st (crochet)			ssk	(sl 1 knitwise) 2 times; place sts back onto left needle and knit the stitches together through back loops = 1 stitch decreased; left-leaning decrease
cm	centimeter(s)	p	purl		
CO	cast on	p2tog	purl 2 sts together = 1 st decreased		
dpn	double-pointed needles	pm	place marker		
est	established (i.e., work as set up)	psso	pass slipped stitch(es) over	st(s)	stitch(es)
in	inch(es)	rem	remain(s)(ing)	St st	stockinette stitch (British = stocking stitch)
k	knit	rep	repeat		
k2tog	knit 2 sts together = 1 stitch decreased; right-leaning decrease	rnd(s)	round(s)		
		RS	right side	tbl	through back loop(s)
		sc	single crochet (British = double crochet)	WS	wrong side
				wyb	with yarn held in back
m	meter(s)			wyf	with yarn held in front
mm	millimeters	sl	slip	yd	yard(s)
		sl m	slip marker	yo	yarnover
		sk2p	sl 1, k2tog, pass slipped st over = 2 sts		

YARN, KNITTING NEEDLES, AND GAUGE

YARN

Every pattern in this book can be made with many types of yarn. The yarn used to make the projects in the photographs was more or less randomly chosen. You can work with any yarn you like—just make sure the gauge will produce something in the size you have in mind.

Because it can be difficult to find a suitable yarn, I recommend that you take this book with you to the yarn store so you can get help finding a good choice of yarn from among those available.

Before the pattern instructions, you'll find a list of materials that includes the yarn I used for that project; if you'd like to use those same yarns, more information about where you might be able to find them is at the back of the book. However, each pattern also lists the yarn content and weight, and a gauge, to make it easy to substitute other yarns that work up similarly.

COTTON YARN

Many of the items in this book are knitted with cotton yarn. Most often a fine cotton, but some, such as potholders, are worked with a heavier, sturdier cotton. Cotton's characteristics mean it doesn't felt or pill, which is good for smooth surface projects that will be on the dining table or decorating something in the house. Cotton yarn is especially good for toys, particularly for children who are so small that they put every toy in their mouths. It's more and more common to find organic cotton yarn, so look for it at your local yarn store if you're interested in trying it.

WOOL YARN

In this book, you'll also find many projects designed for wool yarn. I've used various types of wool yarns for the knitted garments in the book, depending on their purpose.

• *Wool yarn for felting*: Knitted items that are felted acquire a firm, soft, and fine surface. If they're knitted in a pattern, the motifs will contract a bit. Yarn suitable for felting is 100% non-superwash wool, alpaca, or a blend of the two fibers. If a wool yarn is good for felting, the ball band will often make a note of it.

• *Durable wool yarn*: For socks, mittens, and other garments that will need to tolerate hard use, you can choose yarn that is specially processed for durability. These yarns are often blended with synthetics for extra strength.

• *Washable wool yarn*: Many of today's washing machines have a special program for washing fabrics very gently, to approximate hand-washing. If your washer doesn't have such a program, you should choose a superwash-processed yarn. That yarn goes through a chemical process to prevent it from shrinking or felting in the washing machine.

YARN AMOUNT

The yarn amounts listed in each pattern are for the yarn I used for the projects in the photographs. If you're knitting with a different yarn, you may need a little more or a little less of it than I did.

KNITTING NEEDLES

Knitting needles of many different types and qualities are available. Choose a needle size that suits the yarn you're working with to obtain the gauge you need for the project. But make sure your needles are a material and weight you like to knit with. Good needles are worth their weight in gold.

• *Set of double-pointed needles with 5 needles:* These are used when you'll be knitting around on projects that don't have enough stitches to fit around a circular needle. The stitches are divided as evenly as possible onto 4 needles and the 5th is used for knitting. Double-pointed needles come in various lengths and you should choose the length which best suits your project.

• *Circular needle:* A cable with a needle tip at each end. These are used for larger projects that are knitted in the round, but you can also use them to knit back and forth over many stitches. The length of the cable varies depending on what you want to knit. For a hat, a circular about 16-20 in / 40-50 cm long is recommended.

GAUGE

In order for your project to be the same size as that given in the pattern, you have to knit at the same gauge. Make a gauge swatch or measure as you work to be sure your gauge is correct.

Lay the measuring tape on the knitted fabric and count how many stitches are in 4 in / 10 cm. That number of stitches is the gauge. The drawing below shows a gauge of 18 stitches in 4 in / 10 cm.

Begin by choosing the yarn and needles you think will produce the correct gauge. Knit a swatch or measure as you work. Check the gauge. If the count is too low, try a smaller needle; if it is too high, choose a larger size.

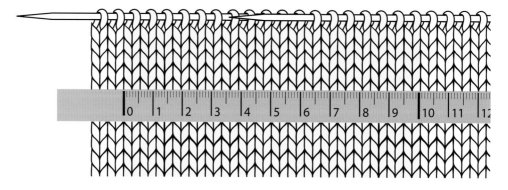

POMPOMS

Christmas should be lavish and lovely, so it's natural that you'll want to indulge in a few pompoms to embellish your knitting!

You can find plastic pompom makers at a yarn or craft store. Or you can make your own templates for the sizing you want.

Wrap yarn around a flat or round template (for example, a bottle or a stiff card) of the right size, at least 100 times—you'll have a thick bundle. Carefully remove the bundle from the template. Then wrap a long, loose strand around the bundle several times and tie it very securely. With one end of that strand, sew several times though the center of the bundle from all sides, until it's firm and you're sure the pompom won't loosen later on.

Cut all the loops around the pompom smoothly with sharp scissors, and then sew in the ends of the wrapping strand.

I-CORD

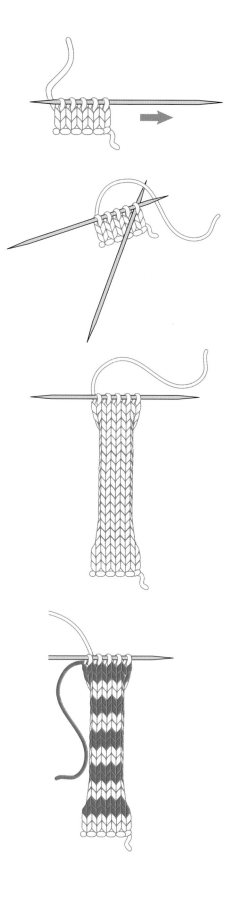

Here's how to make a wide, solid cord that can be used for a little of everything. You can use I-cord for ties for a hat, mittens, or stockings, or as a hanging loop for a Christmas stocking.

Cords can be useful in and of themselves, too—why not knit a cord for your eyeglasses, or as a bracelet?

I-CORD CONSTRUCTION

This is a straightforward, easy method. The result is a flat, thick cord.

An I-cord is worked with 2 double-pointed needles. Cast a few stitches onto one needle. Work with 3-7 stitches—just try it to see what the right number is for the cord size you want.

Cast on the stitches and knit 1 row. *Do not turn the work; instead, slide the stitches to the right tip of the needle. Bring the yarn behind the stitches, tighten a little, and knit across again.* Repeat from * to * until the cord is desired length. Bind off.

TWO-COLOR I-CORD

You can knit I-cords with more than one color. Just make sure you don't lose the strands inside the cord. This makes an especially solid cord that won't stretch in length if it gets snagged.

FRINGE AND HAIR

Some of the designs in this book use fringe. Tight rows of fringe are also used for dolls' hair. A row of fringe perks up a knitted garment and lifts it to new heights. You can also use a different yarn for the fringe than that for the garment, which makes an interesting contrast.

HOW TO MAKE A FRINGE

Cut the yarn into strands a little more than twice the length you want for the fringe. Insert a crochet hook between two stitches in the knitted fabric and pull a strand through so the ends hang loose; even them out if necessary.

Fringe for hair: First, make a ring of fringe that will fit all around the head where the hair will be attached. Throughout, insert the crochet hook in from the bottom up. Hair's usually done with a fine yarn, which means you can work with two strands held together. If you're using a heavier yarn, though, you can skip over stitches in the head baseline now and then. Fill the entire head with fringe, working upward from the bottom.

FELTING

In order for something to felt, it must be worked in non-superwash, pure wool. Felting causes the fibers in the knitted piece to cohere; the surface becomes tighter and softer, and the whole piece shrinks and becomes smaller.

In general, there are two ways to felt.

FELTING BY HAND
Submerge what you want to felt in warm, soapy water. You can use a regular hand soap or hair shampoo. Traditionally, a "green soap" was used for felting, but it doesn't smell very nice. Always protect your hands with heavy gloves when felting, especially with very hot or boiling water.

Take up the garment and knead it hard against a washboard or another ridged surface. Twist and knead the piece on the wrong side. If you want to speed up the process, you can felt using boiling water. Keep working until you feel that the piece is felted enough.

When you felt by hand, you have complete control over the process and amount of shrinkage. For example, you can choose to felt the thumbs of mittens to make them smaller than the rest of the mittens. Felting also makes it easier to shape the piece well.

The disadvantage with felting by hand is that it can be strenuous and tedious, particularly when a large item must be felted thoroughly.

FELTING IN THE WASHING MACHINE
Put the items to be felted in the washing machine with a hand towel. Add a tablespoon of green soap or liquid wool wash. Wash at 86°F/30°C. The result can vary quite a lot from one washing machine to another. Small items tend to felt only a little in the washing machine, so wash them together with something else.

AFTER FELTING
Shape the felted piece while it's still wet. Dry flat. If you want a slightly fuzzy surface, brush the piece all over with a nail brush.

PATTERN INSTRUCTIONS

ADVENT

Advent is a time of waiting—we are waiting for Christmas to come—but it's also a busy time in and of itself. There are all kinds of events: Christmas parties, end-of-season festivities, Christmas tables full of cheer. A nice item for everyone is an Advent calendar. It counts the days down, and at the same time there's a little gift or surprise every day. These days, it isn't just children who'd be happy to have a calendar—everybody enjoys having something nice to look forward to each day. Four Sundays before Christmas, we light the first Advent candle, and each week until Christmas we light another. The anticipation is part of the season.

A new tradition in Norway is *rampenissen*, mischievous elves who fly into the house and make trouble every night all through the Advent season. Anyone who finds such an elf in the house has their hands full.

For those of us who are happy to knit, the Advent season is a great time. What could be better than sitting in front of the fireplace on a dark, cold night before Christmas, with your knitting in your hands? The first patterns in this book are for items just for Advent.

ADVENT CALENDAR BAGS

Make every day of Advent exciting!

There are no rules for what an Advent calendar should look like. It can, for example, look like a dresser with 24 drawers, or a large picture with 24 hooks to hang packages on; it can be digital, or it can be a scratch card.

Here you'll find instructions for 24 different gift bags, all with charming motifs. You can fill the bags with small surprises. Set them up on a table or shelf, hang them up on a hook or branch, or fill a basket with them.

Dates aren't worked into these bags, so you'll need to add a small tag for each so the recipient will know which day to open it. You can make your own date tags or tie on tags as in the pictures. I used a variety of ribbons from Panduro (a Scandinavian craft store) to tie the bags.

SKILL LEVEL
Experienced

FINISHED MEASUREMENTS
Length: Approx. 4¾ in / 12 cm
Circumference: Approx. 9¾ in / 25 cm
If you want longer bags, you can knit a few extra rounds between the pattern and the eyelet round.

MATERIALS
Yarn:
CYCA #1 (fingering) Søstrene Grene Anna & Clara (100% cotton, 175 yd/160 m / 50 g).

Yarn Amounts and Colors:
This yarn is sold in 50 g balls without color numbers. Shops usually stock a variety of assorted colors depending on the season. For these bags, I used 1-2 balls of White, and then less than 1 ball of Red, Dark Blue, Dark Green, and Turquoise. Buy any colors you like, but remember to get extra of whatever color you're using as a base color.

Substitute Yarn: Yarn for a gauge of 26-28 stitches in 4 in / 10 cm. If you use heavier yarn and larger needles, the bags will be bigger.

Needles: U. S. size 1.5 / 2.5 mm: Set of 5 dpn.

Notions: Ribbon or cords, number tags.

GAUGE
Approx. 26 sts = 4 in / 10 cm. Adjust needle size to obtain correct gauge if necessary.

Instructions

All the bags are knitted in the round and worked following the same basic pattern. You can use the blank chart if you want to draw designs for your own special bag.

① CO 16 sts with the color on the lower part of the chart chosen for the bag you want to knit. Divide the sts evenly onto 4 dpn = 4 sts per needle. Join to work in the round.

② Increase 2 sts on each needle as indicated on the chart. After the initial increase rnd, increase 2 sts on each needle on every other rnd until there are 14 sts on each needle = 56 sts total.

③ **Motif section:** Work the motif as shown on the chart for the bag you are knitting.

④ After completing the motif, work 5-6 rnds with the main color before the eyelet rnd. If you want a longer bag, add more rounds at this point.

⑤ Make an eyelet round for the ties.

⑥ Work 5 rnds in stockinette after the eyelet rnd and then BO. The top edge will roll down naturally.

FINISHING
Use the cast-on yarn tail to close the hole at the bottom of the bag. Weave in all ends neatly on WS. Draw a cord/ribbon through the eyelets, and the bag is ready to be used.

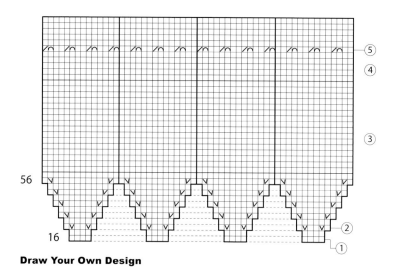

Draw Your Own Design

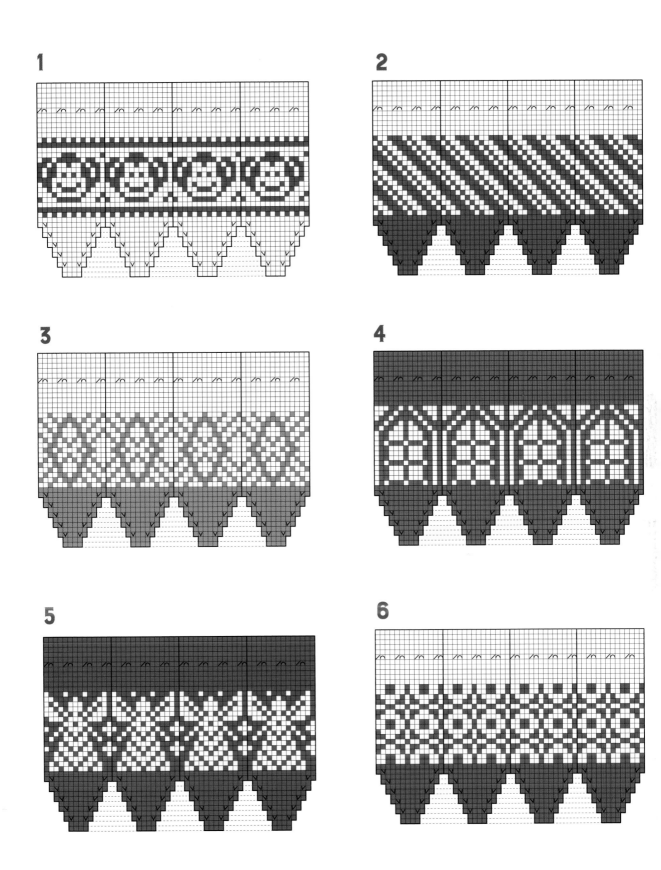

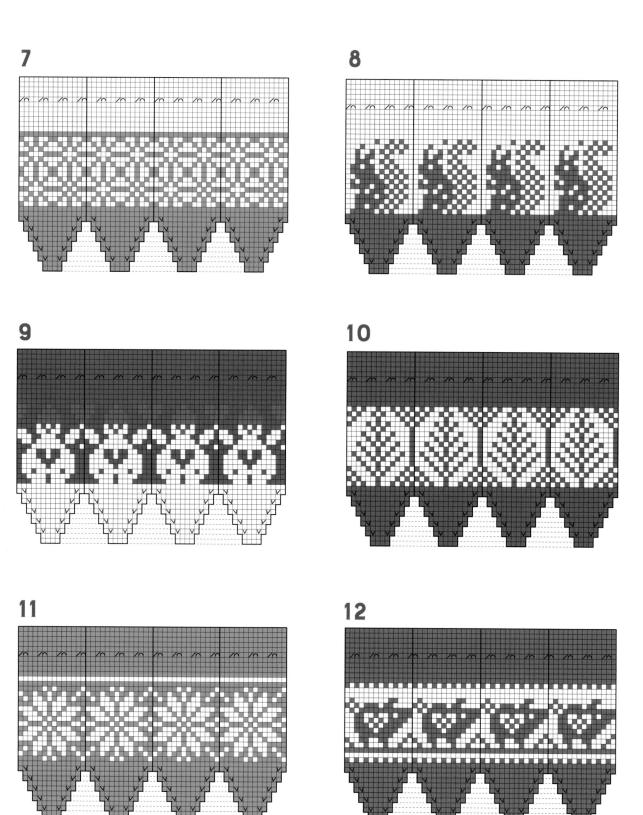

13

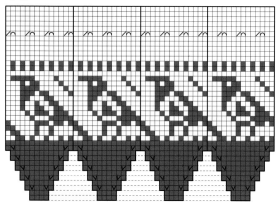

14

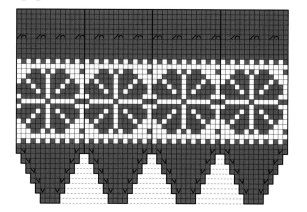

15

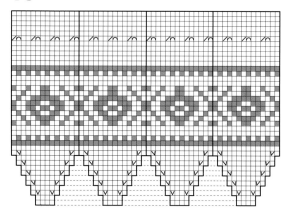

16

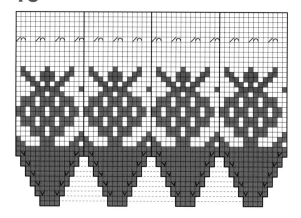

17

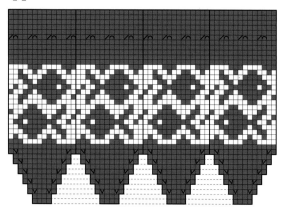

18

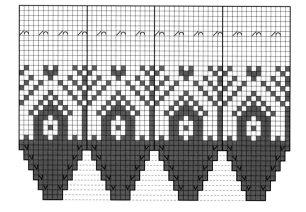

19

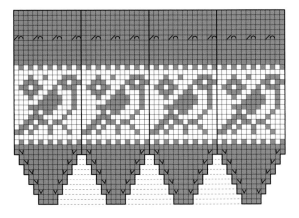

20

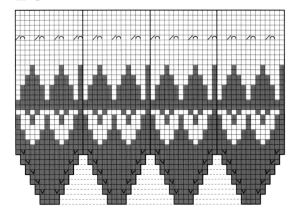

21

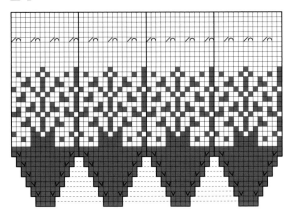

22

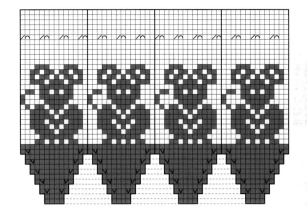

23

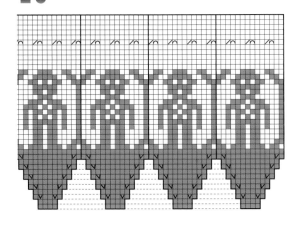

24

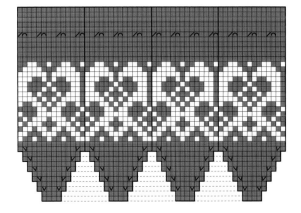

DOLLS

A doll isn't just decorative—it can also be fun to play with and, in the best case, become a dear friend. It's easy to be happy with soft, huggable dolls, and they're always ready to play!

Here you'll find patterns for three dolls. Even if the dolls are different in both looks and character, they're all the same size and knitted following the same basic pattern. You'll also find instructions for clothing to give each doll personality.

Let your imagination run wild and knit the dolls a whole wardrobe, if you like!

RAMPUS RAMPENISSE

Instead of the traditional Advent calendar with gifts every day during Advent, in many homes in Norway it's common to let a *rampenisse*—a particularly troublesome sort of elf—fly into the house and live there for all of December. This elf makes trouble all night, and it's fun and exciting to get up early in the morning to see what on earth has gone wrong each day! These days, it's increasingly common to buy a so-called "Elf on the Shelf" doll and let it play the role of the *rampenisse*. But you can also knit your own rambunctious Rampus *rampenisse* with a character all its own.

LITTLE POSTMAN

While Rampus contemplates tricks, his kind friend goes about looking for positive things worth noting. The Little Postman has a small backpack containing letters describing all the lovely things he's seen over the course of the day. When evening arrives, he delivers his letters to their recipients—comforting words, compliments, and praise for good deeds can all be shared by the postman.

DOLL WITH HAIR

The body for this doll is knitted following the same pattern as for the *rampenisse* and the Little Postman, but the whole doll is made in a single color. This doll has a thick head of hair that can be styled with knitted hair or fringe. You can make the hair as long or short as you want, in whatever color you like.

Our doll became an angel doll, but don't be fooled! The wings are only attached at the back of the dress, and when they're removed the doll is completely ordinary. You'll find patterns for several outfits on the following pages, too, to make it easy to knit a personalized doll that's just right for the recipient.

SKILL LEVEL
Experienced

FINISHED MEASUREMENTS
Total length of the doll is approx. 17¾ in / 45 cm.

MATERIALS
Yarn: All three dolls as well as all of their clothes and accessories (except for the angel doll's hair) are knitted with Søstrene Grene's Anna & Clara [CYCA #1 (fingering), 100% cotton, 175 yd/160 m / 50 g].

Yarn Amounts and Colors:
This yarn is sold in 50 g balls without color numbers. Shops usually carry a variety of assorted colors depending on the season. The yarn is both reasonably priced and has good yardage/meterage, so you won't need more than one ball of each color, no matter which doll or which of the small garments you choose to knit.

For the Rampus doll, you'll need 4 colors of yarn: a color for the skin, Red, White, and Dark Green.

For the Little Postman: a color for the skin, White and Blue yarn.

The doll with hair is knitted only in whatever color you've chosen for her skin. Make her following the same charts as for the other dolls but only with that color. For her hair, you can use some fine wool yarn. We used Viking of Norway's Nordlys, color 927.

Substitute Yarn: Naturally, the dolls can be made with other wool yarns, or another kind of yarn, if you like. If you use heavier yarn and larger needles suitable for it, the dolls will be bigger.

Needles: U. S. size 1.5 / 2.5 mm: set of 5 dpn.

Notions: Non-allergen and flame-resistant fiberfill. We used Panduro white filling.

GAUGE
Approx. 28 sts = 4 in / 10 cm. The dolls should be knitted firmly so the fiberfill won't poke out through the stitches. Make sure there are no large openings, especially along the edges near decreases. Go down a needle size or two if you're knitting so loosely there are gaps between the stitches. Adjust needle size to obtain correct gauge if necessary.

DOLLS

Instructions

The dolls are knitted in the round, beginning at the top of the head and all the way down to the feet. The arms are knitted separately, filled, and then sewn on.

① Work following the chart *Head*. The chart shows the number of stitches on each needle and repeated the same way 4 times around. With skin color, CO 12 sts. Divide the sts evenly onto 4 dpn = 3 sts on each needle; join and pm for beginning of rnd. Knit 2 rnds.

② Increase on every other rnd as shown on the chart until there are 15 sts on each dpn = 60 sts total.

③ Repeat the chart row marked with 3 a total of 20 times.

④ Decrease 2 sts on each dpn on every other rnd as indicated on the chart until 5 sts rem on each needle = total of 20 sts rem.

⑤ **Neck:** Rep this round 5 times.

⑥ Now continue to the chart for the *Body*. The chart is repeated 2 times around; the front and back of the doll are knitted the same way. Increase on the 1st rnd and then on every 4th rnd as shown on the chart until there are a total of 15 sts on each dpn = 60 sts total.

⑦ Knit the stomach for a total of 27 rnds without increasing or decreasing.

⑧ Decrease 2 sts on each side of the doll (on Ndls 1 and 3) as shown on the chart to form the hip. Rep every 4th rnd as indicated on the chart.

⑨ Last rnd for the body: BO the 9 sts at center front and 9 sts on center back.

⑩ Continue working, following the *Foot* chart. Knit across 13 sts on one side, increase 1 st at inside of thigh = 14 sts on this rnd. Continue around. Place the sts for the other leg on a holder. Work 52 rnds for the leg. For the Rampus doll, work 30 rnds with Green and 22 rnds with skin color for the leg.

⑪ **Heel:** Make sure the heel is centered at the center back—it's easy to make a mistake here! Decrease 1 st at each side until 12 sts rem.
Next rnd: K6, turn and purl 5 sts; turn.
   Work back and forth with 1 st less for each row. When 2 sts rem, continue working back and forth but with 1 more st for each row. To avoid holes at the sides of the heel for each row, pick up and knit 1 st before the last st and knit it together with the last st.

⑫ Knit 5 rnds over all the sts.

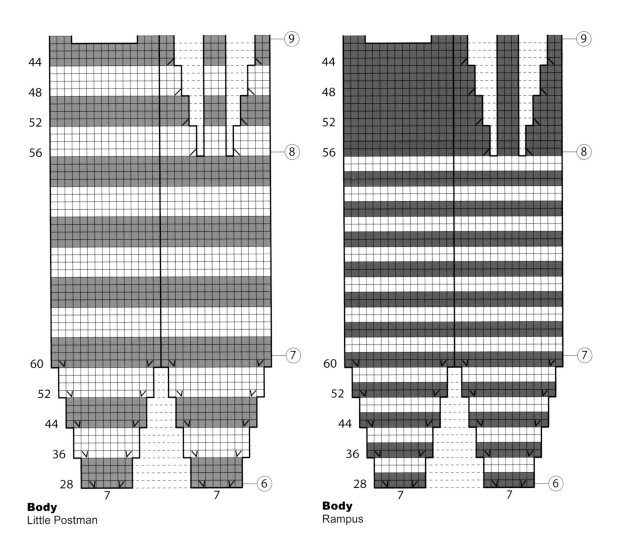

Body
Little Postman

Body
Rampus

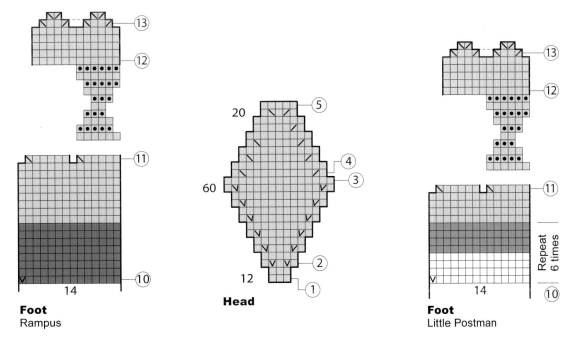

Foot
Rampus

Head

Foot
Little Postman

Repeat 6 times

⑬ Decrease 2 times at each side. Cut yarn and draw end though rem st. Make the other leg the same way.

⑭ Now work from the *Arm* chart. The arms are worked from the shoulder down. CO 6 sts and work back and forth.

⑮ Increase 1 st on each side on every 4th row.

⑯ When there are a total of 15 sts, join to work in the round. Work a total of 52 rnds to the thumb.

⑰ **Thumb:** Place the first 2 sts and the last 2 sts of the round on a holder. Continue over the rem sts for 4 rnds.

⑱ BO as shown on the chart. Seam the top of the hand.

Thumb: Place a needle through the 4 sts and k4. Cut yarn and draw end through rem sts.

Make the other arm the same way.

FINISHING

Turn the doll inside out and weave in all ends on the WS. Turn right side out. Fill the doll with the fiberfill, beginning at the head. Stuff in small amounts at a time to prevent the filling from clumping. Fill until the doll feels firm or else the head will flop about. Fill in the entire body and both feet. Seam the crotch.

Turn the arms inside out and weave in ends on WS. Use the yarn ends to close any openings at the thumb, if necessary. Turn right side out and fill. Sew the arms securely to the body, centered at the sides.

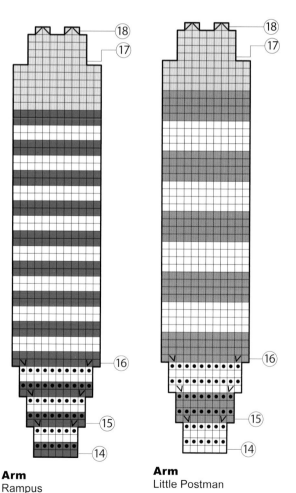

Arm
Rampus

Arm
Little Postman

The dolls have fine features which are made only with yarn.

Nose: Sew three stitches with the face color—sew back and forth and back again over the 2 sts at the center of the face. Center the nose between the top of the head and the neck.

Eyes: Make a "knot" by wrapping the yarn 6 times around a stitch. Sew each end down into the doll's face, aligned symmetrically around the nose (see photo).

Mouth: Sew two stitches with red yarn (see photo). Sew the ends of the yarn directly into the head and attach them so they're hidden under the hat or hair.

HAIR AND ACCESSORIES FOR THE DOLLS

HAIR

(See also page 17)

Knit the doll and complete the finishing. Cut the yarn for the hair double the desired length. Use a crochet hook to add fringe all around the hairline. Insert the hook from the top, behind the strand between two stitches. Pull a yarn strand through the stitch. Make a fringe for each stitch. Fill the edge all around the hair line and then continue upwards to the next row.

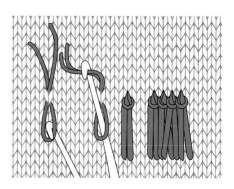

SCARF

The scarf is worked back and forth horizontally with a circular U. S. size 2.5 / 3 mm.

CO 75 sts and knit back and forth in garter st for 10 rows (= 5 garter ridges). BO.

BIB

The little postman wears a little bib, which is knitted back and forth with Light Blue yarn.

SUSPENDERS

Rampus likes to wear pants with suspenders. Cross cotton ribbon suspenders over the back and stitch to the body with sewing thread. Sew a button to each front end of the suspenders.

Instructions

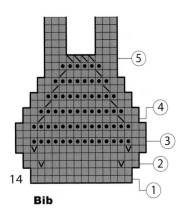

Bib

---

① CO 14 sts. Knit back and forth, beginning with 1 garter ridge.

② Increase 1 st at each side 2 times as indicated on the cart.

③ Now work in stockinette with knit on the RS and purl on the WS except for the first and last 2 sts of every row which continue in garter st. Rep until there are a total of 18 St st rows on the front of the bib.

④ Decrease at each side as shown on the chart, a total of 4 times, until 10 sts rem.

⑤ K3, BO 4, k3. The last 3 sts continue as an I-cord strap (see page 16). Place the first 3 sts of row on a holder. Knit until strap is long enough; cut yarn and draw end through rem sts. Make the strap on the opposite side the same way.

HATS

Instructions

The hats are knitted in the round.

① CO 60 sts. Divide the sts onto 4 dpn with 15 sts on each needle; join to work in the round. Work following the Hat chart. Work the chart repeat around, beginning with the k2, p2 ribbing for 6 rnds.

② Continue with the stripe pattern on the chart.

③ Decrease 2 sts on each dpn on every 4th rnd as shown on chart. Continue to end of chart. Cut yarn and draw end through rem sts. Tighten and weave in ends neatly on WS. Sew the hat to the doll's head.

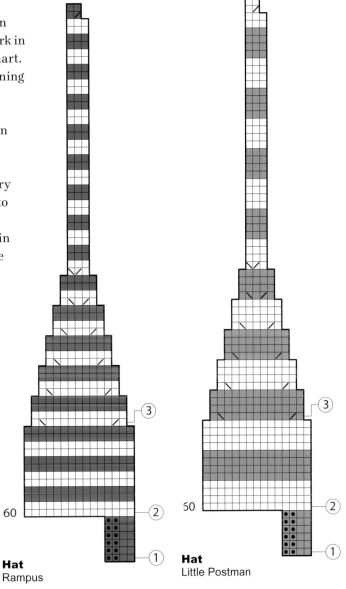

Hat
Rampus

Hat
Little Postman

SLIPPERS

Knit some slippers for the dolls to keep their little feet warm.

Instructions

The slippers are worked back and forth and then seamed on the bottom and up the back afterwards.

① CO 19 sts. Work following the *Slippers* chart. Knit back and forth in garter st for 10 rows (= 5 ridges).

② With contrast color (CC), knit 2 rows (= 1 ridge).

③ Now continue knitting back and forth but with 1 st less on each row (= short rows – knit until 1 st less than previous row; turn). Leave unworked sts on needle. When 3 sts rem, cut yarn.

④ **Sole:** With CC, knit across all sts for a total of 5 rows.

⑤ BO the 1st st, k6, BO 1, k7, BO 1.
Fold the piece. Seam the sole and back of slipper.

Make the second slipper the same way.

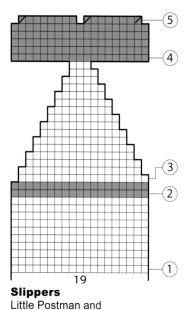

Slippers
Little Postman and
Doll with Hair

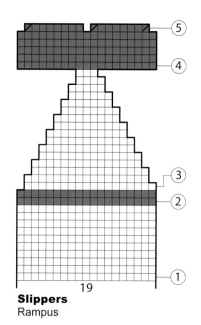

Slippers
Rampus

BACKPACK

Naturally, the Little Postman needs something to carry letters in. This backpack is worked in the round from the bottom up, with the flap worked last.

Instructions

① Work from the *Backpack* chart. CO 16 sts. Divide the sts evenly onto 4 dpn (= 4 sts per dpn) and join to work in the round. Knit 2 rnds.

② Increase 2 sts on each needle on every other rnd as shown on the chart until there are 10 sts on each needle or 40 sts total.

③ Rep this rnd 22 times.

④ **Edge:** Work knit and purl pattern at the sides and front of the backpack as shown on the chart.

⑤ **Eyelet rnd:** Work eyelet rnd following chart. After working the eyelet rnd, work 2 more rnds of the edge pattern.

⑥ BO 26 sts at the sides and front as shown on the chart. The rem sts continue as the flap.

⑦ Now work the *Flap* chart. The flap is worked back and forth over the 14 rem sts. Always knit the first and last 2 sts of

every row. The center sts are worked in St st. Rep the 1st two rows 7 times until there are 14 rows on the flap.

⑧ BO at each side of the flap on every other row as shown. Continue following the chart and then BO the rem sts. Do not cut yarn. With crochet hook, ch 4 and attach the other end of the sts to the other side of the flap.

Straps: CO 5 sts and make an I-cord (see page 16). BO when the cord is approx. 15 in / 38 cm long. Attach the center of the cord to the backpack, at the center back below the flap. Attach an end at each side at the bottom of the pack.

Cord: On each side of the opening, attach a cord by drawing it through the eyelet rnd; knot at center front. The cord can be crocheted or twisted with yarn, or, use a narrow ribbon.
Seam the opening at the base. Weave in all ends neatly on WS. Sew on a button.

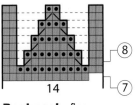

Backpack, flap

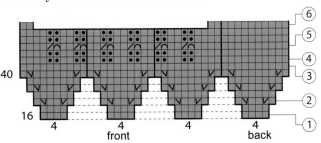

Backpack

VEST

Rampus is wearing green pants, so a vest of the same color matches perfectly!

Instructions

The entire vest is worked back and forth.

① CO 60 sts. Work following the *Vest* chart. Knit 6 rows (= 3 garter ridges).

② Continue in St st, *but* always knit the first and last 4 sts of every row. Work 26 rows.

③ Knit one front, placing rem sts on a holder: With RS facing, k14; turn and purl back. Decrease at each side on every other row as indicated on the chart. Complete the front as shown on the chart. BO.

④ **Back:** Begin by binding off the next 4 sts and then work back over next 26 sts. Decrease at each side on every other row as indicated on the chart. Complete the back as shown on the chart. BO.

⑤ **Opposite front:** BO the next 4 sts and work front to correspond to opposite side.

Join shoulders. Weave in all ends neatly on WS.

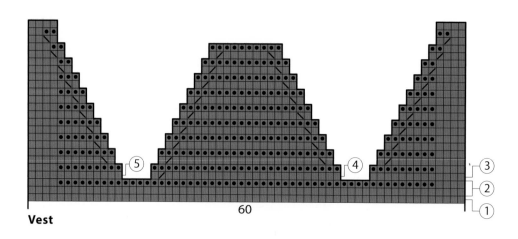

Vest

60

DRESS WITH WINGS

The dress is easily knitted in the round with a colorwork pattern around the chest and a lace skirt. The straps join at the back neck.

Instructions

① CO 66 sts and join to work in the round. (You might want to join after working the first row.) Work following the *Dress* chart. Rep the pattern around. The dress begins with 2 white ridges and then 1 blue ridge (1 ridge = 2 knit rows).

② Continue around following the chart.

③ Increase to 88 sts by working a yarnover after every 3rd st.

④ **Lace rnds:** Rep these 2 rnds (bracketed and labeled with 4 on chart) until you've worked 46 lace rnds or until skirt is desired length.

⑤ Finish with 2 ridges with White. BO.

"HALTER NECK" STRAPS
Pick up and knit 9 sts on one side of front, positioned so there will be 9 sts between straps at center and 9 sts on opposite side of front. Make sure the straps will be evenly centered on the front. Work strap back and forth on 2 needles.
On RS: Knit across.
On WS: K2, p5, k2.
Continue as est until strap measures 6¼ in / 16 cm. BO. Make the second strap the same way. The straps are used to support the angel wings.

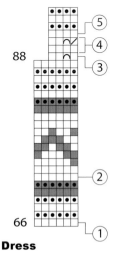

Dress

WINGS

Each wing is knitted separately. A wing is worked back and forth, folded double along the center and sewn together at the sides so they'll be sturdy. Each wing is worked from the bottom tip and up.

Instructions

① Work following the *Wing* chart. CO 5 sts. Work back and forth in garter st.

② Now increase 2 sts on every other row by making a yarnover on each side of the center st. Continue increasing as est until there are 45 sts total.

③ Next, decrease 2 sts on every other row with 1 decrease before and 1 after the yarn over at each side of the center st.

④ Now also decrease 1 st at each side on every other row as shown on the chart.

⑤ Continue decreasing until 17 sts rem. Knit 1 row and then BO.
Fold the wing in half down the center and loosely sew the sides together. Make the second wing the same way.

Attach each wing to the corresponding strap end on the dress. Sew on two small snaps so the straps are joined at back neck.

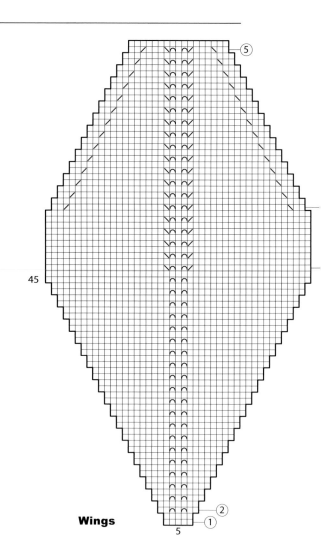

Wings

PANTS

The dress will look nice with short pants worn underneath. The same pattern can be used for long pants—just knit longer legs. The pants are worked with a set of 5 double-pointed needles.

Instructions

The pants are worked from the top down. CO 60 sts. Divide the sts onto 4 dpn and join to work in the round. Work 3 rnds of k1, p1 ribbing and then continue in St st for 2½ in / 6 cm.

Work one pant leg: Knit 4 rnds over 30 sts for one side. Place the rem sts on a holder for the other leg. BO 2 sts on the inside of the leg on every 4th rnd until 22 sts rem. Knit 4 rnds.

Eyelet rnd: Work 1 eyelet rnd (yo, k2tog) around.

Knit 4 more rnds and then BO.

Work the second leg the same way.

Fold the bottom edge of each leg along the eyelet rnd and sew down edge on WS. Seam the opening between the legs.

FINALLY, CHRISTMAS

Although Advent is a lovely season, we're certainly
very happy when we open our eyes on the morning
of December 24 and know that Christmas is
here! It's twice as good because we know the pre-
Christmas stress is over and there's nothing left but
to enjoy Christmas as thoroughly as we can.

CHRISTMAS STOCKINGS

When I was a child, the Christmas stocking was absolutely the one stocking we went for first. It was taken out on the evening of December 23rd ("little Christmas Eve") and hung up over the stove or at the foot of the bed frame. During the night the stocking was mysteriously filled with Christmas candies and other delights. The stocking typically held a Christmas booklet, rolled up and crammed into the stocking. The center of that rolled booklet was filled with goodies—for example, an orange, a little box of raisins, chocolate, and caramels, and maybe even a packet of chewing gum.

Over the past few years, it's become more common to make special Christmas stockings. Each child in the family gets a personalized Christmas stocking, which can then be used every year. The stockings are decorated with pretty Christmas motifs in bright colors, and they're much bigger than a regular stocking so they have plenty of room inside.

But Christmas stockings aren't necessarily only for children! Why not surprise an adult friend with a special stocking on Christmas Eve morning? A lovely gift for the Christmas houseguest or for a totally new acquaintance. With a name panel and motifs to suit the recipient, a Christmas stocking is a wonderful gift. And an empty Christmas stocking can easily hang on the wall as a decoration so everyone can enjoy it through the whole holiday season.

Here are patterns for five different Christmas stockings. If none of the designs are exactly what you want, you can use the template to design your own. All these Christmas stockings have a name panel at the top. If you don't know who might get the stocking, you can omit the name and knit in "Merry Christmas," the year, or something else instead.

These stockings are knitted with wool yarn and then felted in the washing machine. For information on felting, see page 18. You can, of course, knit the stockings with your choice of yarn, and you don't have to felt them, either.

SKILL LEVEL
Experienced

FINISHED MEASUREMENTS
After felting, my stockings were:
Total Length: Approx.15¾ in / 40 cm
Leg and Foot Width: Approx. 5½ in / 14 cm

MATERIALS
Yarn: CYCA #3 (DK/light worsted)
Sandnes Garn Mor Aase Ullgarn (100% wool, 100 yd/ 91 m / 50 g).
Substitute Yarn: Yarn that can be felted and is recommended for 22-24 sts in 4 in / 10 cm, with needles U. S. sizes 4-6 / 3.5-4 mm.
Yarn Amounts and Colors:
1 ball of each recommended color for each stocking.
Needles: U. S size 6 / 4 mm: Set of 5 dpn.
Crochet Hook: U. S. size G-6 / 4 mm for pompom ties.

Instructions

With White, CO 60 sts. Divide the sts onto 4 dpn, with 15 sts on each needle. Join to work in the round; pm for beginning of rnd. Begin with the facing: Knit 7 rnds. The facing will be folded in later and sewn down on the WS. Continue, following the chart for the stocking you want to knit.

① **Eyelet rnd:** Work following the chart. After working eyelet rnd, continue following the charted pattern.

② **Name panel:** Fill the panel as you like. Charts for the alphabet, numbers, and a blank chart are all on page 68.

③ Continue following the chart to the heel, which is indicated with a heavy, dark line. Cut yarn.

④ Work the **Heel** chart. The heel is worked back and forth over the 30 sts at center back. Place the rem sts on a holder for the instep. Use the heel color on the chart for your pattern choice. Begin at the 1st st on needle 4 (15 sts before the beginning of the rnd).
Row 1 (RS): K30 with heel color.

⑤ Turn and p29.

⑥ Turn and k28. Continue the same way, with 1 less st on each row. The sts not worked now should remain at each side of the needle.

⑦ Continue the short rows until 15 sts rem at the center of the heel. Now work back and forth in St st with 1 st more on each row.
RS: Knit the last st tog with the next st. To avoid holes along the increase line, M1 in the strand before the next st.

⑧ **WS:** Purl across, purling the last st tog with the first "waiting" st.
M1p in the strand before the next st.
Continue as est until all 30 sts of the heel have been worked. Cut yarn.
Now return to chart for Christmas stocking.

⑨ **Foot:** The pattern begins at the center of the heel. Complete pattern and cut yarn.

⑩ **Toe shaping:** The Pony and Teddy Bear on Skis Christmas stockings are knitted with a long toe shaping while the other designs have short toes. Choose the one you want. Follow either the *Long* or *Short Toe* chart.

Use the same yarn color as for the heel. Begin at the side of the stocking and repeat charted pattern twice around.

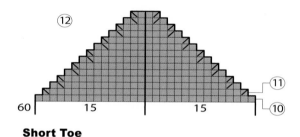

Short Toe

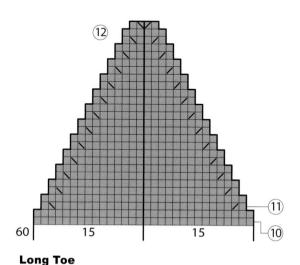

Long Toe

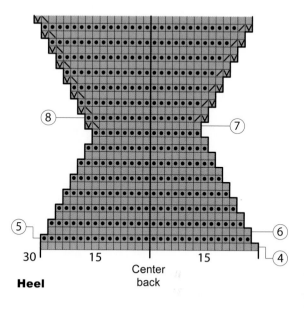

Heel

Center back

⑪ Decrease at each side at shown on the chart. The long toe is decreased on every other rnd while the short version decreases on every rnd, but alternates with 2 or 0 sts between the decreases at the sides on every other rnd.

⑫ Cut yarn and draw through rem sts. Weave in all ends neatly on WS. Fold facing at eyelet rnd and sew down loosely on WS.
Felt the stocking following instructions on page 18.

POMPOMS FOR THE STOCKINGS
The Christmas stockings in the photos have two yarn pompoms each. The pompoms are attached at each end of a cord crocheted with chain stitches. Fold the cord double and sew it securely at the back of the stocking so it sticks up into a hanging loop (see photo, page 58).

JONAS

These young deer have moved away from the herd a bit so they can gaze wonderingly at the Christmas star.

MAIN COLOR: White.
PATTERN COLORS: Light and Dark Blue, Dark Red. The heels and toes are worked in Red.

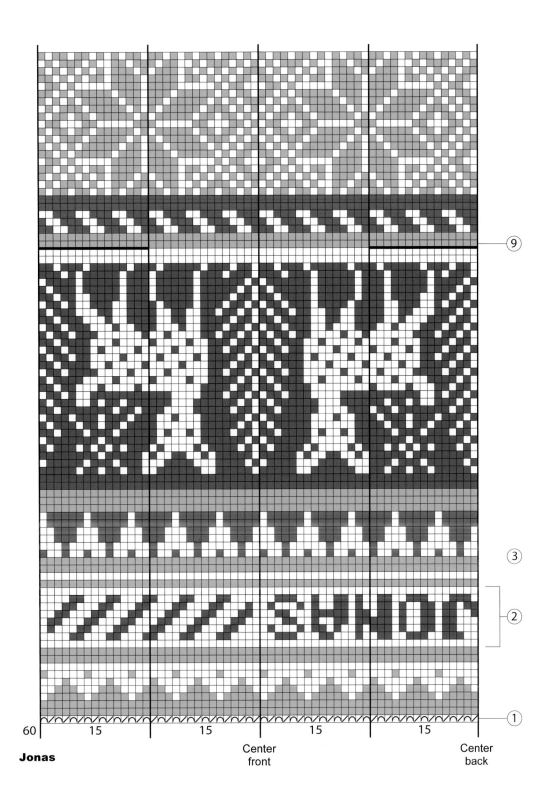

Jonas

MARTIN

The dancing elves are a motif that will reappear later in this book. Here they've freed the reindeer, now on a wild flight across the plateau. The elves themselves have let loose in a wild polka dance.

MAIN COLOR: White.
PATTERN COLORS: Light and Dark Blue, Dark Red. The heels and toes are worked in Dark Blue.

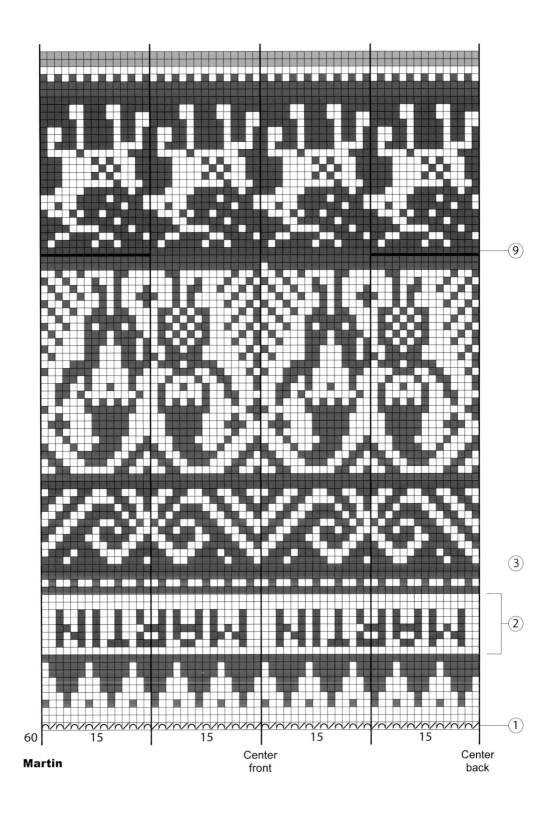

Martin

60 15 15 15 15

Center front

Center back

PONY

There are lots of kids who'd love to find a real pony under the Christmas tree on Christmas Eve. Not everyone can have that wish granted, of course, but a stocking with a pony motif isn't a bad substitute!

The pony stocking is knitted with White as the main color with Pink, Yellow, and Light Blue as pattern colors. Instead of a name, the pony panel substitutes the year in the text panel.

MAIN COLOR: White.

PATTERN COLORS: Pink, Yellow, and Light Blue. The heels and toes are worked in Light Blue.

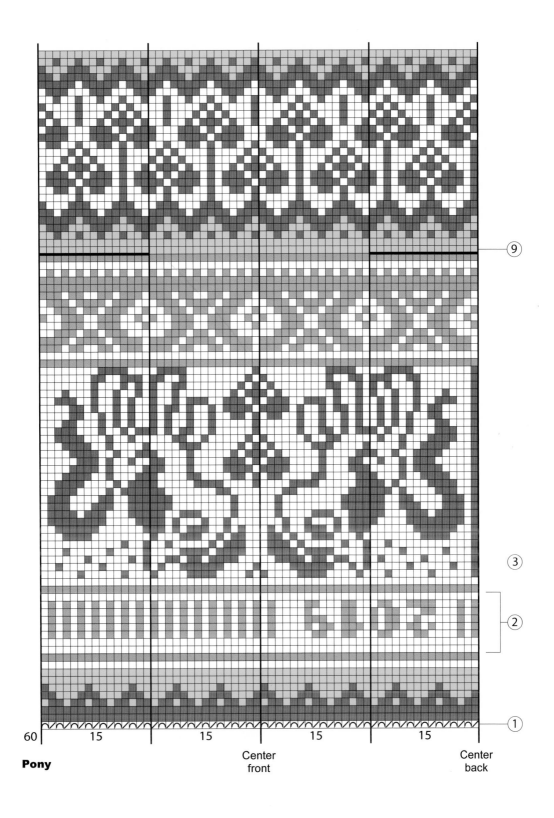

60 | 15 | 15 | 15 | 15

Pony

Center front

Center back

TEDDY BEAR ON SKIS

It would be great to find a pair of skis under the Christmas tree. The teddy bear on the stocking has had a good run of luck this year and is out trying the skis for the first time.

MAIN COLOR: White.
PATTERN COLORS: Light and Dark Blue, Pink. Teddy's scarf is knitted with White and then the Pink is added later with duplicate stitch. The heels and toes are worked in Pink.

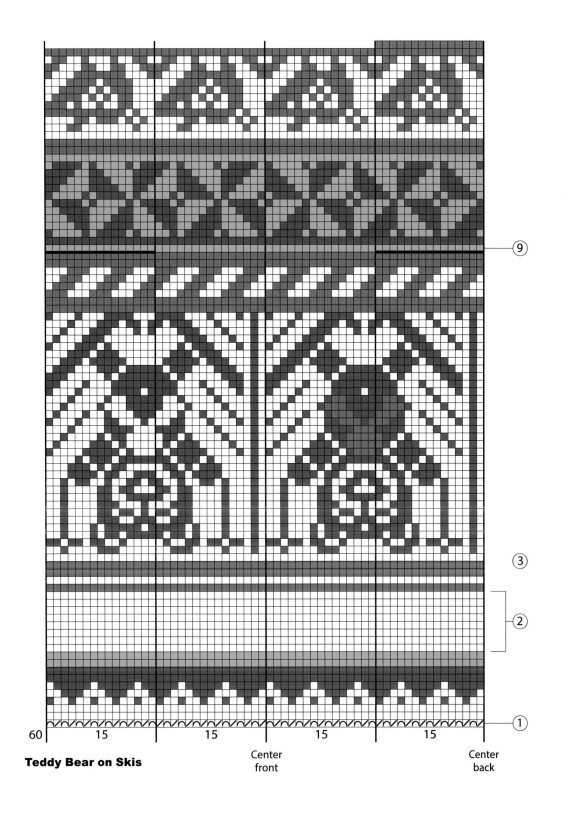

Teddy Bear on Skis

60 | 15 | 15 | 15 | 15

Center front

Center back

⑨ ③ ② ①

BIRGITTE

You'll meet these little bullfinches in several places in this book. They show up for the first time on this Christmas stocking. These red birds light up the cold winter landscape in Norway and create a beautiful Christmas mood.

MAIN COLOR: White.
PATTERN COLORS: Light and Dark Blue, Dark Red. The heels and toes are worked in Light Blue. The bullfinches are knitted with Red and then the Black and Grey accents are added later with duplicate stitch.

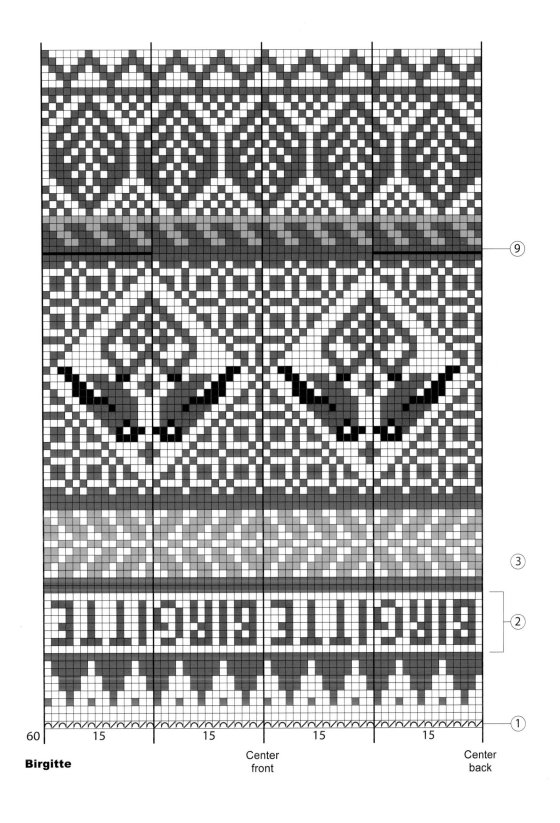

Birgitte

60 | 15 | 15 | Center front 15 | 15 | Center back

NAME PANEL

Alphabet and Numbers

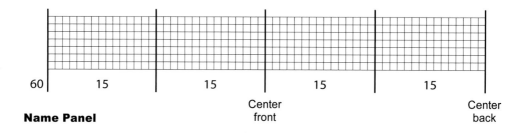

Name Panel

60   15   15   15   15

Center front   Center back

DESIGN YOUR OWN CHRISTMAS STOCKING

Perhaps you want to feature a special motif on
your stocking? Here's an empty chart so you
can draw in your own patterns.

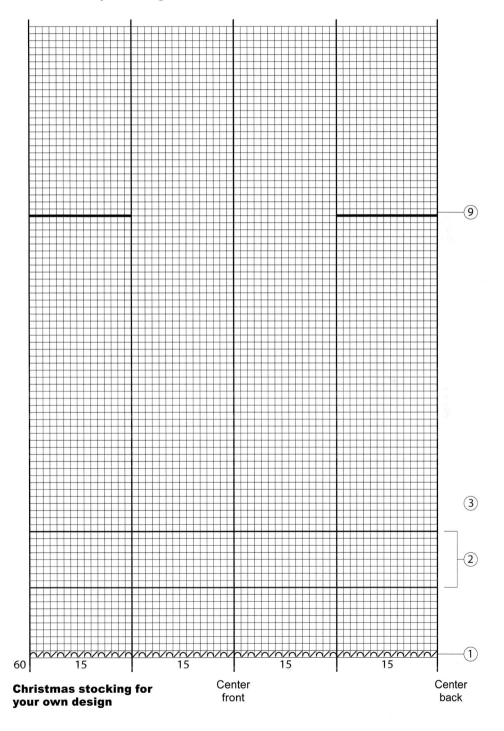

**Christmas stocking for
your own design**

THE CHRISTMAS TABLE

On Christmas Eve, we carefully set the table and serve the tasty Christmas dinner. It is important to follow traditions, but of course every family has their own specific ideas about what should be cooked and how it should be presented.

No matter what's included on the menu, though, it's such a pleasure to be able to set the table with something special that day. It's especially nice to decorate the table with handmade items, creating just the right setting for your family's special traditions.

POTHOLDERS

Imagine standing in front of the stove and preparing Christmas dinner. Perhaps you need a pair of new potholders that are pretty and practical? Potholders also make lovely Christmas gifts that anyone can use, and they'll add luster to any Christmas kitchen.

These potholders are knitted in the round with two strands per round to make them extra thick. They can also serve as a hot pad for the table. Either way, there's a bonus: you can hang them on the kitchen wall as a fun Christmas decoration.

PIGS ON THE RUN

In Scandinavia, pigs appear as motifs on Christmas paper and cards all the time; they're a traditional Christmas image. So why not knit pictures of our pink friends on potholders? These lively pigs managed to escape the Christmas platter at the last second. The potholders, worked with white, pink, and red yarn, set the mood for Christmas at the stove.

SKILL LEVEL
Experienced

FINISHED MEASUREMENTS
Width: Approx. 8¾ in / 22 cm
Length: Approx. 8¼ in / 21 cm

MATERIALS
Yarn:
CYCA #3 (DK/light worsted) Rauma PT Petunia (100% cotton, 120 yd/110 m / 50 g).
Yarn Amounts and Colors for 1 potholder:
60 g White 296, 20 g Pink 245, 15 g Red 256.
Substitute Yarn: Cotton yarn recommended for needles U. S. sizes 2.5-6 / 3-4 mm at 20-22 sts in 4 in / 10 cm.
Needles: U. S. size 2.5 / 3 mm: 16 in / 40 cm circular.
Crochet Hook: U. S. size D-3 / 3 mm

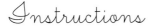

The potholder is knitted in the round and edged with two rounds of single crochet.

① With White, CO 96 sts. Join, being careful not to twist cast-on row. Pm for beginning of rnd. Work following the *Pigs on the Run* chart. The chart is worked twice around. Pm with 24 sts between each, corresponding to the vertical lines on the chart to make it easier to follow the pattern.

② Complete charted rows and then BO. Weave in ends neatly on WS.

CROCHETED EDGING

Begin at the corner for the hanging loop. Work sc all around edge of potholder. Bring the yarn through the outermost stitch loop on each side of the opening at the top and bottom of the potholder. At the sides, crochet through the stitch at the side edge.

Rnd 1: Work (5 sc, sc2tog) around, but work 3 sc in each corner.

Rnd 2: Turn work and work 1 sc in each sc around + 2 sc in each corner.

HANGING LOOP

Ch 7 in the corner and join at corner. Work 12 sc around loop. Fasten off.

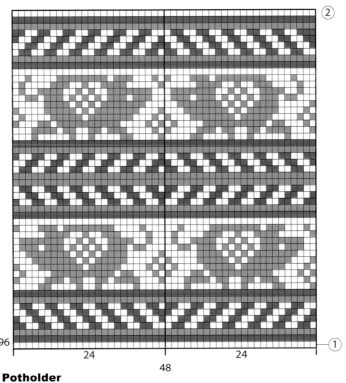

Potholder
Pigs on the Run

GINGERBREAD HOUSE

Make your kitchen especially cozy in the days before Christmas with this sweet potholder, shaped like a gingerbread house.

What can be better when baking for Christmas than using handmade potholders? These potholders can also serve as hot pads for any dishes on the table. And of course these fine gingerbread houses are Christmas decorations in and of themselves, and can hang on a hook all through the holidays.

SKILL LEVEL
Experienced

FINISHED MEASUREMENTS
Width: approx. 7½ in / 19 cm
Length: approx. 8 in / 20 cm

MATERIALS
Yarn:
CYCA #3 (DK/light worsted) Rauma PT Petunia (100% cotton, 120 yd/110 m / 50 g).
Yarn Amounts and Colors:
For 1 potholder: 25 g Reddish Brown 257, 25 g White 296
Substitute Yarn: Cotton yarn recommended for needles U. S. sizes 2.5-6 / 3-4 mm at 20-22 sts in 4 in / 10 cm.
Needles: U. S. size 2.5 / 3 mm: 16 in / 40 cm circular and set of 5 dpn for top of house.
Crochet Hook: U. S. size D-3 / 3 mm.

Instructions

The potholder is knitted in the round.

① With White, CO 96 sts. Join, being careful not to twist cast-on row. Pm for beginning of rnd. Work following the *Gingerbread House* chart. The chart is worked twice around. Pm with 24 sts between each, corresponding to the vertical lines on the chart to make it easier to follow the pattern.

② Begin decreasing at each side as indicated on the chart. When the sts do not fit around the circular, change to dpn.

③ At the roof tip of the house, k3tog twice. Cut yarn and weave in ends neatly on WS.

Seam the house at the base.

HANGING LOOP
Ch 7 at the tip of the roof and join at same place. Work 12 sc around loop. Fasten off.

Potholder
Gingerbread House

WINTER BIRDS

These two small bullfinches have landed yet again, this time on a pair of potholders.

FINISHED MEASUREMENTS
Width: approx. 8 in / 20 cm
Length: approx. 7 in / 18 cm

MATERIALS
Yarn:
CYCA #3 (DK/light worsted) Rauma PT Petunia (100% cotton, 120 yd/110 m / 50 g).

Yarn Amounts and Colors:
For 1 potholder: 20 g Red 256, 24 g White 296 + a small amount of black and gray embroidery yarn for the bullfinches. Cotton embroidery thread also works well.
Substitute Yarn: Cotton yarn recommended for needles U. S. sizes 2.5-6 / 3-4 mm at 20-22 sts in 4 in / 10 cm.
Needles: U. S. size 2.5 / 3 mm: 16 in / 40 cm circular.
Crochet Hook: U. S. size D-3 / 3 mm.

Instructions

The potholder is knitted in the round and edged with two rounds of single crochet. The bullfinches are knitted with red yarn. The gray and black areas are embroidered on with duplicate stitch before the edging is crocheted around the potholder.

① With White, CO 88 sts. Join, being careful not to twist cast-on row. Pm for beginning of rnd. Work following the *Winter Birds* charts—the birds on the front and the star pattern on the back. Pm with 22 sts between each, corresponding to the vertical lines on the chart, to make it easier to follow the pattern.

② Complete charted rows and then BO. Weave in ends neatly on WS. Using duplicate stitch, embroider each bird with black and gray yarn as shown on the chart.

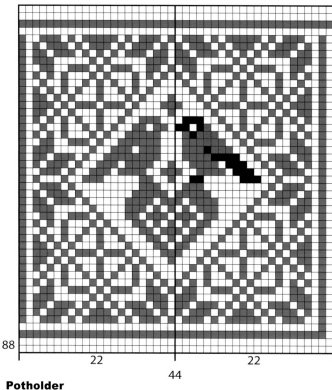

Potholder
Winter Birds, front

88

22   22

44

CROCHETED EDGING

Begin at the corner for the hanging loop. Work sc all around edge of potholders. Bring the yarn through the outermost stitch loop on each side of the opening at the top and bottom of the potholder. At the sides, crochet through the stitch at the side edge.

Rnd 1: Work (5 sc, sc2tog) around, *but* work 3 sc in each corner.

Rnd 2: Turn work and work 1 sc in each sc around + 2 sc in each corner.

Since the potholder isn't very big, you may want to add more rounds of sc.

HANGING LOOP

Ch 7 in the corner and join at corner. Work 12 sc around loop. Fasten off.

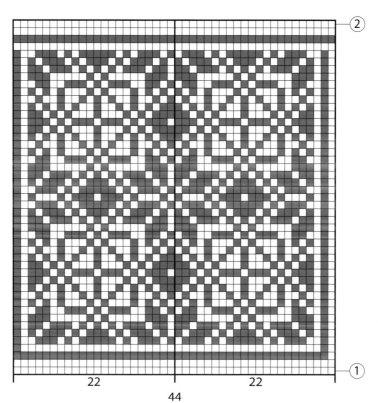

Potholder
Winter Birds, back

SILVERWARE HOLDERS

This year we can decorate the Christmas table with these fun and inviting little holders for napkins and silverware. You can place spruce twigs between them for extra Christmas spirit!

You can lay a house or a tree at every place setting, or you can set out the Christmas buffet and line the silverware holders in a row like a street, and let the guests pick up their own utensils.

It's not easy to make the right angles for the corners on the houses—they can quickly turn into rounded corners and then tilt the edges of the door and windows. But that'll be part of their charm. Do you have some fun decorations to hang on their walls? The styling is only limited by your imagination.

These silverware holders can do more than one job, too: they can also decorate the walls.

All the houses are knitted back and forth. The windows and doors are knitted in stockinette, with the purl stitches on the wrong side of the work. The colors in the windows are embroidered with duplicate stitch over the knit stitches with yarn in a contrast color.

The door and window frames are crocheted on with white yarn. Insert the hook into the work and bring a loop up. Insert the hook down into the next stitch, draw up a loop, and pull that loop through the first loop (slip stitch). Continue with slip stitches around.

Alternatively, embroider the frames using a tapestry needle and chain stitch.

For the window frames, sew a cross in the window with white yarn and long straight stitches. In the center of the cross, sew a small stitch on each side so the thread is secured.

For the edging, the pieces of the houses are crocheted together with single crochet, and, if there is a roof, it will have a crocheted edging. Crochet all around each house. Join the parts with a basting thread before you crochet to prevent the structure from becoming too crooked.

SKILL LEVEL
Experienced

MATERIALS
Yarn:
CYCA #3 (DK/light worsted) Gjestal Cotton Sport (100% cotton, 110 yd/101 m / 50 g).
Yarn Amounts and Colors:
One ball of each color (see photos) is enough for several holders.
Substitute Yarn: Cotton yarn recommended for 23 sts in 4 in / 10 cm.
Needles: U. S. size 2.5 / 3 mm.
Notions: Tapestry needle for embroidery.
Crochet Hook: U. S. size D-3 / 3 mm.
Notions: To decorate the holders: small plastic beads, metal bells for the church bells, and a heart-shaped button for the door.

HOUSE WITH WOOD SIDING AND A ROUNDED ROOF

Instructions

The front, back, and roof, are each
worked separately. The front and back
are worked lengthwise while the roof is
worked on the diagonal and sewn to the
top of the back. We used violet yarn for
the front and dark red for the roof. White
yarn accents the house.

NOTE: 1 garter ridge = knit 2 rows.

① CO 30 sts and work following the
chart for *House with Wood Siding, front.*

② Work 5 garter ridges and then
stockinette for the window and door—
purl on the WS as indicated on the chart.
Continue in garter and stockinette until
there are a total of 10 garter ridges.

③ Knit 5 more ridges and then BO.

④ **Roof:** CO 20 sts. Work the roof back
and forth, following the chart *House with
Wood Siding, roof.* Knit 3 garter ridges.

⑤ Decrease to shape the roof as shown
on chart. There are 3 garter ridges
between each decrease.

⑥ Shape sides, decreasing on every other row.

⑦ Cut yarn and draw end through 2 rem sts.

BACK WALL

Work as for the front, omitting the window/door. CO 30 sts, knit 15 ridges, BO.

Embroider the window grilles with long horizontal and vertical stitches and small stitches at the center to secure embroidered lines.

Crochet or embroider the chain-stitch frames around the window and door (see page 83).

FINISHING

Securely sew the roof to the back wall. Crochet the edges all around the house: Place the front over the back and pin or baste the pieces together. Beginning at the front, work in sc all around the outer edges of the house, making sure the yarn goes through both layers.

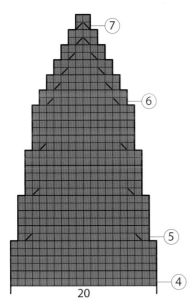

House with Wood Siding,
roof

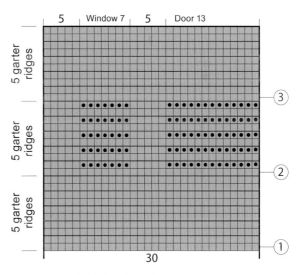

House with Wood Siding,
front

GINGERBREAD HOUSE

Instructions

This house is made in two pieces that are later crocheted together. We used brown yarn for the house, white for the trim, and red for the window. Begin with the front, which is worked from the bottom up.

NOTE: 1 garter ridge = knit 2 rows.

① CO 18 sts. Work following the *Gingerbread House, front* chart. Work in garter st ridges except for the door and window which are worked in stockinette over the 6 center sts. Work 20 rows (10 ridges) with the door.

② Knit 8 rows (4 ridges) of the wall.

③ Work 14 rows (7 ridges) with the window.

④ Knit 8 rows (4 ridges) above the window. Cut Brown.

⑤ Knit 2 rows (1 ridge) with White and then BO.

⑥ Work following the chart *Gingerbread House, back wall and roof.* CO 18 sts and knit a total of 60 rows (30 ridges).

⑦ Decrease 1 st at each side on every 3rd ridge as shown on the chart. Cut yarn and draw end through 2 rem sts.

FINISHING

Use red yarn to work duplicate stitch over the stitches at the center of the window. Crochet or embroider (see page 83) the chain-stitch frames all around the door and window. Embroider the window frames with long horizontal and vertical stitches and small stitches at the center to secure the embroidered lines. Crochet the edges all around the house: Place the front over the back and pin or baste the pieces together. Beginning at the front, work sc all around the outer edges of the house, making sure the yarn goes through both layers.

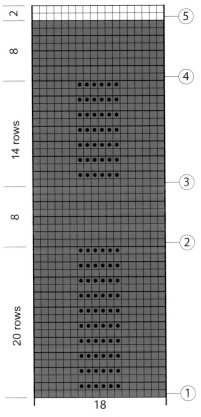

Gingerbread House,
front

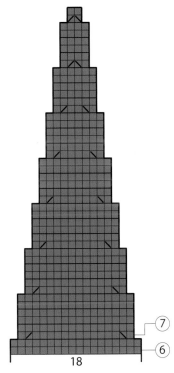

Gingerbread House,
back wall and roof

CHURCH

Instructions

The church is built in two sections that are crocheted together. The church is knitted with white yarn, with brown outlining the door and window, and a bit of leftover red yarn for duplicate stitching the window.
Begin at the front, which is knitted from the bottom up.
NOTE: 1 garter ridge = knit 2 rows.

① CO 18 sts. Work following the *Church, front* chart. Work in garter stitch, except for the door, which is worked in stockinette over the 10 center sts. Knit 18 rows (9 ridges) for the height of the door.

② Knit 8 rows (4 ridges) for the wall above the door.

③ Knit 14 rows (7 ridges) with the window in stockinette (the window narrows at the top).

④ Knit 12 rows (6 ridges) above the window. BO.

⑤ Work the back following the *Church, back wall and roof* chart. CO 18 sts and knit 60 rows (30 ridges).

⑥ Decrease 1 st at each side and then on every 3rd ridge as shown on the chart. Cut yarn and draw end through rem 2 sts.

FINISHING

Use Red to work duplicate stitch over the window stitches. With Brown, work chain st (see page 83) around the door frame and then embroider with straight stitch for the center of door. Also with Brown, work chain stitch along the top of the window and then embroider the cross with straight sts. Secure the cross with short sts at the center. Use White to embroider the window frames (with long and short lines as for the cross).

Crochet the edges all around the church: Place the front over the back and pin or baste pieces together. Beginning at the front, work sc all around the outer edges of the church, making sure the yarn goes through both layers. With Brown, work 10 sc at each side of the rooftop. The church holder shown here is decorated with a couple of tiny bells in the "belfry."

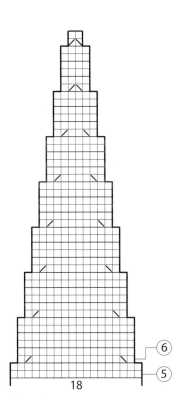

Church,
back wall and roof

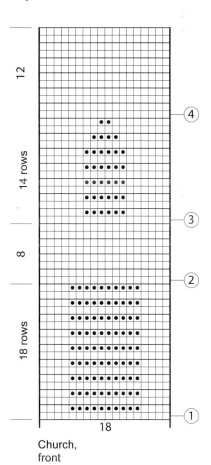

Church,
front

CHRISTMAS BLOCK HOUSE

Instructions

The Block silverware holder is knitted in two pieces that are then crocheted together. Red and green blocks alternate for the house. Dark green and dark red are used for the windows, white trimming the building, windows, and door.
Begin at the front, which is knitted from the bottom up.
NOTE: 1 garter ridge = knit 2 rows.

① With Red, CO 18 sts. Work following the *Christmas Block House*, front chart. Work in garter stitch except for the door, which is stockinette over the 6 center sts. Knit 14 rows (7 ridges) for the height of the door.

② Knit 4 rows (2 ridges) for the wall above the door.

③ Cut Red and continue with Green. Knit 2 ridges.

④ Knit the window in stockinette over the center 6 sts. Continue to top of chart, changing colors as indicated, and then BO.

⑤ Work following the *Christmas Block House, back wall* chart: With Green, CO 18 sts and work a total of 56 rows (28 ridges), changing colors as indicated on chart.

⑥ Work to top of chart and then BO.

FINISHING

Use yarn in a contrast color to work duplicate stitch over the stitches of the two windows. Work chain st (see page 83) all around the door and windows. Embroider the window frames with long horizontal and vertical stitches and small stitches at the center to secure the embroidered lines. Crochet the edges all around the house: Place the front over the back and pin or baste the pieces together. Beginning at the front, work sc all around the outer edges of the house, making sure the yarn goes through both layers.

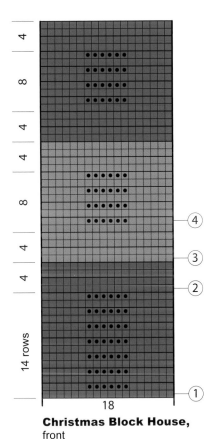

Christmas Block House,
front

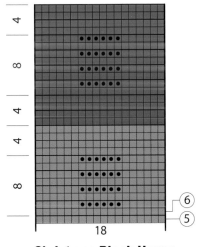

Christmas Block House,
back wall

SEED STITCH COTTAGE

Instructions

This house is knitted in two pieces which are then crocheted together. I used red and white yarn with a tiny bit of brown for the chimney and some dark red for the duplicate stitch over the window. Begin at the front, which is knitted from the bottom up.

NOTE: Seed stitch alternates knit and purl every row. On RS: K1, p1; WS: Work purl over knit and knit over purl.

① With Red, CO 18 sts. Work following the *Seed Stitch Cottage, front wall* chart. Work in seed stitch, except for the door, which is worked in stockinette over the 6 center sts. Knit 20 rows for the height of the door.

② Knit 6 rows for the wall above the door.

③ Work 8 rows in seed st, except for the window, which is worked in stockinette over the 6 center sts.

④ Work 10 rows in seed st above the window. Cut Red and attach White.

⑤ With White, knit 4 rows (2 ridges) and then BO.

⑥ Make the back wall: With White, CO 18 sts and work following the chart for Seed Stitch Cottage, back wall and roof. Knit 56 rows (28 ridges).

⑦ Decrease 1 st at each side and then on every 6th row as shown on the chart. Work to en of chart and BO

FINISHING

Use a contrast color yarn to work duplicate stitch over the stitches of the window. Work chain st (see page 83) all around the door and windows. Embroider the window frames with long horizontal and vertical stitches and small stitches at the center to secure the embroidered lines. Crochet the edges all around the house: Place the front over the back and pin or baste the pieces together. Beginning at the front, work sc all around the outer edges of the house, making sure the yarn goes through both layers.

CHIMNEY

With Brown, pick up and knit 4 sts centered at the rooftop. Knit 4 ridges (8 rows); cut Brown. With White, knit 2 ridges (4 rows) and then BO.

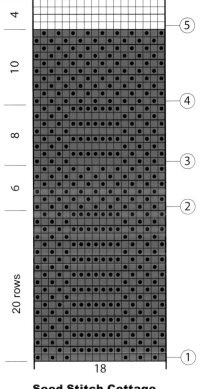

Seed Stitch Cottage,
front wall

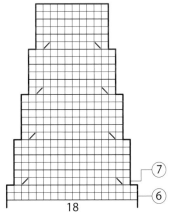

Seed Stitch Cottage,
back wall and roof

CHRISTMAS TREE

The Christmas tree coordinates well with the winter houses. To decorate the tree, I found some neon plastic beads. The delightful little presents underneath the tree were knitted using a variety of techniques. The tree is worked back and forth in garter stitch, from the top down.

The tree is knitted with dark green and brown yarn. The presents are wrapped (knitted) with red, white, and light green.

① CO 3 sts. Work following the *Christmas Tree* chart. Knit 6 rows (3 ridges). On the next row, increase 1 st on each side with a yarnover after the first st and another yo before the last st. Continue following the chart, increasing 2 sts as est on every 3rd ridge.

When there are a total of 19 sts, knit 4 ridges before the next increase to 21 sts.

Knit 5 ridges to the next increase to 23 sts.

Knit 6 ridges to the next increase to 25 sts.

Knit 7 ridges and then BO.

"The pocket" to hold the silverware is worked back and forth in garter st. With Brown, CO 16 sts and knit 4 ridges for the "trunk". Change to Green and knit 16 ridges. BO.

Sew the trunk to the tree along the lower edge and the sides.

PRESENTS

Light green present: CO 6 sts and work 6 rows in stockinette (knit on RS and purl on WS). BO.

White present: CO 6 sts and work back and forth in seed st for 6 rows:

Row 1: (K1, p1).

Following rows: Work knit over purl and purl over knit.

BO.

Red package: CO 7 sts knit back and forth in garter st for 4 ridges. BO.

Ribbons: Use the yarn to make a cross around the package. Sew down with two small stitches at the crossing point as for the windows on the houses. Tie the packages to the tree with the yarn ends.

Christmas tree decorations: Sew a bead into each hole made by the yarnover increases at the sides of the tree.

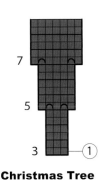

Christmas Tree

PIG

In the old days, the centerpiece of the Christmas table was an entire small pig, baked, holding an apple in its mouth. Today, it's more pleasant—and easier—to decorate the table with a few small homemade pigs. This cheerful pig is knitted with cotton yarn and serves as a table decoration as well as on the Christmas tree. If there are children in the house, you can be sure they'll play with the little pink charmer. Make plenty, so everyone can have one!

SKILL LEVEL
Intermediate

MATERIALS
Yarn:
CYCA #1 (fingering) Søstrene Grene Anna & Clara (100% cotton, 175 yd/160 m / 50 g).

Yarn Amounts and Colors:
1 ball of Pink or another skin color will make at least 2 pigs.
Needles: U. S. size 1.5 / 2.5 mm: Set of 5 dpn.
Crochet Hook: U. S. size E-4 / 3.5 mm for the tail.
Notions: Fiberfill; two small glass beads for the eyes.

GAUGE
The pig should be knitted firmly so the filling won't poke out between the stitches. If you knit loosely, use smaller needles.

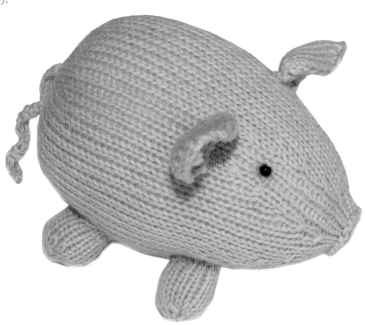

Instructions

The pig is worked in the round from the back to the front.

BODY

① CO 16 sts. Divide the sts evenly onto 4 dpn (4 sts per needle) and join. Work following the *Body* chart. The chart shows the sts on one needle—work the chart a total of 4 times around.

② Increase 2 sts on each needle as shown on the chart. Increase the same way on every other rnd until there are a total of 14 sts on each needle = 56 sts total.

③ Knit 24 rnds without any increasing or decreasing.

④ BO 2 sts on each needle as shown on the chart. Decrease the same way on every 4th rnd until 4 sts rem on each needle = 16 sts total rem.

⑤ **Edge of the snout:** Purl 1 rnd.

⑥ (K2tog) around. Cut yarn and draw through rem sts. Turn the pig inside out and weave in the ends on the inside of the snout.

EARS

The ears, both alike, are worked back and forth.

① CO 4 sts. Work following the *Ears* chart. The ears are worked in stockinette (knit on RS, purl on WS).

② Increase 2 sts on every other row (the RS rows) as shown on the chart until there are a total of 12 sts. Work 5 rows without further shaping.

③ (K2tog) across = 7 sts rem. Purl 1 row and BO on RS.

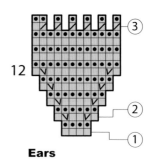

Ears

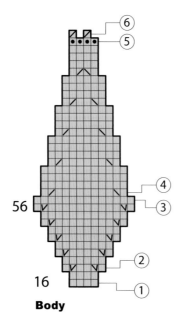

Body

FEET

Make all 4 feet alike. CO 14 sts. Divide the sts onto 4 dpn as evenly as possible and join. Knit 8 rnds. (K2tog) around = 7 sts rem. Knit 1 more rnd. Cut yarn and draw end through rem sts; tighten.

TAIL

Crochet a long chain; turn and work 1 sc in each chain st.

FINISHING

Fill the pig with the fiberfill through the back opening. Thread a strand of yarn around the edge of the opening and tighten; fasten off yarn. Sew on the ears. Fill the feet and sew them to the body. Use sewing thread to sew on the eyes.

CHRISTMAS DECORATIONS
AND SWEET GIFTS

No matter what style your home is, it's so much fun
to go all out for Christmas! You can fill the whole
place to the brim with Christmas spirit. Tables,
chairs, and counters all overflow with everything
that Christmas has to offer, and both expensive
designer items and pretty homemade felted wool
elves have a place.

The Christmas tree can be decorated until it
almost collapses. This year you can cover it with
lovely little knitted items. If there isn't enough room
for everything at home, you'll have some
pretty Christmas gifts—as fun to give as they
are to receive.

SNOWMAN

A snowman with a round stomach, hat, and carrot nose always seems exciting. Hasn't the Christmas snow appeared yet? Don't despair; almost anything can be arranged with a little yarn and some quickly-knitted rows. Snowmen create a winter feeling whether they are toys, hang on the Christmas tree, or look out over the room from a shelf.

The snow-white cotton yarn adds an extra sense of winter and makes the snowman look quite authentic.

FINISHED MEASUREMENTS
Height: Approx. 4¾ in / 12 cm.
Circumference: Approx. 8¾ in / 22 cm.

MATERIALS
Yarn:
CYCA #1 (fingering) Søstrene Grene Anna & Clara (100% cotton, 175 yd/ 160 m / 50 g).
Yarn Amounts and Colors:
1 ball of White will make several snowmen. Use a small amount of Orange for the nose.
Substitute Yarn: Yarn recommended for a gauge of 28-30 stitches in 4 in / 10 cm will make snowmen of the same size as suggested yarn.
Needles: U. S. size 1.5 / 2.5 mm: set of 5 dpn.
Crochet Hook: U. S. size A or B / 2.25 mm
Notions: Fiberfill; small glass beads for the eyes and buttons; needle and thread for sewing on beads.

GAUGE
The snowmen should be knitted firmly so the filling won't bulge out between the stitches. If you knit loosely, use smaller needles (for example, U. S. size 0 / 2 mm).

Instructions

① CO 16 sts. Divide the sts evenly onto 4 dpn (= 4 sts per needle) and join.

Work following the chart *Snowman, body and head*. Knit 2 rnds.

② Increase 2 sts on each needle on every other rnd as shown on chart.

③ Rep this rnd 10 times.

④ Increases for the arms: Increase on every other rnd on the 1st and 3rd needles as shown on chart.

⑤ Work 8 rnds.

⑥ Decrease on every other rnd on the 1st and 3rd needles as indicated on chart.

⑦ **Head:** Knit 20 rnds.

⑧ Shape the top of head by decreasing as shown on chart. Cut yarn and draw end through rem sts. Turn snowman inside out and weave in ends on WS.

FINISHING

Fill the snowman with fiberfill through the bottom opening. Add fill in small amounts at a time to avoid clumping. Use yarn to sew around the opening; tighten and fasten off.

Sew around the neck of the snowman and tighten until the neck looks right.

Sew small stitches down each side and through the snowman to shape the arms.

Sew along the edges of the increase and decrease lines. Fasten off yarn at back neck so it will be hidden by the scarf.

NOSE

The nose is crocheted with orange yarn and a fine hook. Work 5 ch; turn and work 1 sl st into each ch. Sew both ends onto the face so the nose is well-placed. Fasten off yarn at back of neck, under the scarf. Sew on the glass beads (and these will work just as well for the eyes as for the buttons).

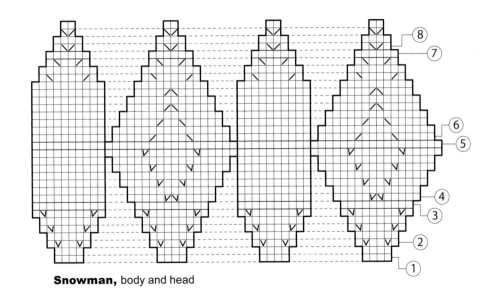

Snowman, body and head

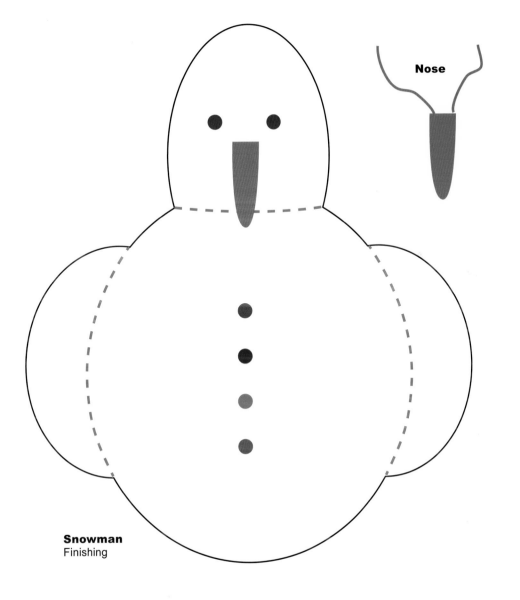

Nose

Snowman
Finishing

HAT AND SCARF FOR THE SNOWMAN

A snowman often sports both a hat and a scarf. It's not unusual to want to give him some clothes; after all, it's so cold standing outside in the snow!

The hat and scarf are knitted with wool yarn, which contrasts nicely with the cotton yarn the snowman is made of.

SKILL LEVEL
Experienced

MATERIALS
Yarn:
CYCA #1 (fingering) Finull PT2 from Rauma Ullvarefabrikk (100% pure new wool, 191 yd/175 m / 50 g).

Yarn Amounts and Colors:
Small amounts of White for the "lice" and pompom + 2 colors that go together well.

Substitute Yarn: Any yarn for a gauge of 26-28 stitches in 4 in / 10 cm.

Needles: U. S. size 1.5 / 2.5 mm: Set of 5 dpn.

GAUGE
To ensure the hat will fit correctly, it should be knitted at the same gauge as for the snowman.

HAT

① With Color 1, CO 24 sts. Working back and forth, knit 6 rows (3 ridges), following the *Snowman's Hat* chart.

② Change to Color 2. Divide the sts evenly over 4 dpn and join to work in the round.

③ Snowflakes: Work the white stitches as indicated on the chart. On the 2nd rnd, purl with white over the previous round's white knit st so the flake stands out.

④ Begin decreasing as shown on the chart.

⑤ Cut yarn and draw end through rem sts; tighten. Seam hat brim. Weave in all ends neatly on WS.

FINISHING

Make a firm little pompom with white yarn and attach it securely to top of hat (see page 15). You can wrap the yarn bundle for the pompom around 3 fingers.

SCARF

The scarf can be knitted either lengthwise or crosswise.

Crosswise Scarf: CO 5 sts. Knit back and forth until scarf is desired length.

Lengthwise Scarf: CO 60 sts. Knit 10 rows (5 ridges). BO.

FINISHING

Weave in all ends neatly on WS. Cross the scarf over the snowman's chest and tack it down with sewing thread and a few stitches.

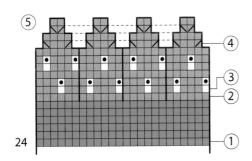

Snowman's Hat

MINI HATS, MITTENS, AND SOCKS

These charming little items are so much fun to knit, and they make pretty decorations—for the Christmas tree, hung on a branch in a vase, or perhaps in a window? They're also perfect for decorating Christmas packages.

It's such a pleasure to sit inside on a dark evening before Christmas and relax with a few of these mini garments, especially because they're so quick to make. In my experience, it's all too easy to binge-knit these small trifles. And they disappear almost as quickly, because everyone wants one!

MINI ELF HAT

This tiny hat makes a nice Christmas decoration, either to hang on the tree or to cover a bottle top.

SKILL LEVEL
Intermediate

MATERIALS
Yarn:
Small amounts of fine wool yarn good for felting. I used CYCA #1 (fingering) Finull PT2 from Rauma Ullvarefabrikk (100% pure new wool, 191 yd/175 m / 50 g) and CYCA #2 (sport, baby) Tove from Sandnes (100% wool, 175 yd/ 160 m / 50 g).
Needles: U. S. size 1.5 or 2.5 / 2.5 or 3 mm: Set of 5 dpn.

Instructions

The White edging is worked back and forth in garter stitch while the rest is worked around in stockinette.

① With White, CO 24 sts. Work following the *Elf Hat* chart: begin by knitting 6 rows (3 ridges) back and forth.

② Change to Color 2: Divide the sts evenly onto 4 dpn and join to work in the round.

③ Begin decreasing as indicated on chart.

④ Cut yarn and draw end through rem sts; tighten. Seam the garter edge of hat brim. Weave in ends neatly on WS. Felt the hat (see page 18). Pat hat into shape and lay flat until completely dry.

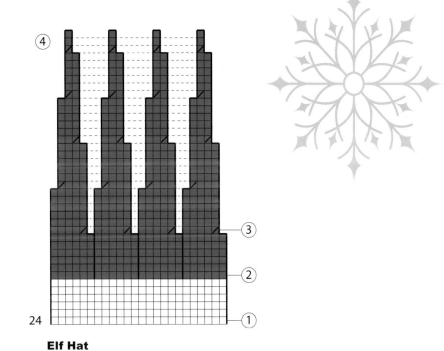

Elf Hat

MINI MITTENS

These tiny mittens can only be worn by the smallest of baby elves. The elf mother also makes them for decorations, either to hang on the Christmas tree or on a wreath she has woven with twigs. You might also find them dangling off the car's rearview mirror or hanging on a key chain. A plain little Christmas package can be spiffed up with some little mittens, too.

SKILL LEVEL
Intermediate

MATERIALS
Yarn:

Small amounts of fine wool yarn good for felting. I used CYCA #1 (fingering), Finull PT2 from Rauma Ullvarefabrikk (100% pure new wool, 191 yd/175 m / 50 g) and CYCA #2 (sport, baby), Tove from Sandnes (100% wool, 175 yd/ 160 m / 50 g).

Needles: U. S. size 1.5 / 2.5 mm: Set of 5 dpn.

Notions: These mittens can be embellished with gold or silver cords as "mitten ties." They might also be decorated with small charms or jewelry elements.

Instructions

① With MC, CO 16 sts. Work following the *Mini Mitten* chart: Knit the first 2 rows back and forth = 1 ridge.

② Divide the sts evenly onto 4 dpn and join to knit in the round. Continue following the chart.

③ **Thumbhole:** With a smooth contrast color yarn, knit the 3 sts marked on the chart—red marks the right-hand thumbhole and blue marks the left. Slide these 3 sts back to left needle and knit in MC. Knit 10 more rnds before shaping the top.

④ Decrease at the sides as shown on chart.

⑤ Cut yarn and draw through rem 4 sts; tighten.

⑥ **Thumb:** Knit around over 2 needles. Insert 1 needle into row below scrap yarn and a second needle in row above scrap yarn. Carefully remove scrap yarn. Work thumb following the chart *Mini Mitten, thumb.*

 Rnd 1: Pick up and knit 1 st on front, at side of mitten. Knit 5 rnds.

⑦ Shape top as shown on chart. Cut yarn and draw end through rem 3 sts; tighten.

FINISHING

Weave in all ends neatly on WS. Felt mittens (see page 18). Stretch mittens into finished shape, lay flat, and leave until completely dry.

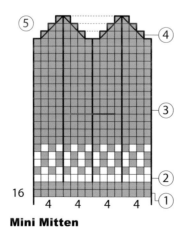

Mini Mitten

Mini Mitten, thumb

MINI SOCKS WITH FLOWERS

For anyone who tends to get very focused on what they're doing, it can be hard to stop knitting these socks. This happens with me when I add patterns to them. I make knitted socks with stripes and motifs, flag socks, and socks with initials. Many of the little sock pairs are given away right after I finish them and become small gifts and decorations.

SKILL LEVEL
Intermediate

MATERIALS
Yarn:
Small amounts of fine wool yarn good for felting. I used CYCA #1 (fingering), Finull PT2 from Rauma Ullvarefabrikk (100% pure new wool, 191 yd/175 m / 50 g) and CYCA #2 (sport, baby), Tove from Sandnes (100% wool, 175 yd/ 160 m / 50 g).
Needles: U. S. size 1.5 or 2.5 / 2.5 or 3 mm: Set of 5 dpn.
Notions: These socks are embellished with gold or silver cords as "stocking bands." They are also decorated with small charms or jewelry elements.

Instructions

① CO 16 sts over 1 dpn. Work following the *Mini Socks with Flowers* chart. Knit 6 rows (3 ridges) back and forth. The rows begin at center back.

② Now divide the sts evenly over 4 dpn and join to work in the round. Continue following the charted pattern, working the leg to the heel in St st with stranded color knitting.

③ The heel is worked back and forth in St st. Knit the first 4 sts.

④ Turn and purl back over the next 8 sts. Leave rem sts on needle or holder for instep. Work 5 rows in St st over the 8 heel flap sts.

⑤ **Rnd 6:** K4, ssk; turn.

⑥ Continue as follows for heel turn:
WS: Sl 1 purlwise, p2tog.
RS: Sl 1 knitwise, ssk.
Rep WS and RS rows until 2 sts rem on heel.

⑦ Now continue in the round. The rnd begins at the center of the sole.
Rnd 1: K1 from heel; pick up and knit 3 sts on side of flap; k8 across instep; pick up and knit 3 sts on opposite side of flap, k1 of heel. Now work the foot as shown on the chart.

⑧ Shape the toe at each side on every rnd as shown on the chart. Cut yarn and draw end through 4 rem sts.

FINISHING
Seam garter st cuff at center back. Weave in all ends neatly on WS. Felt socks (see page 18). Stretch socks into finished shape, lay flat, and leave until completely dry.

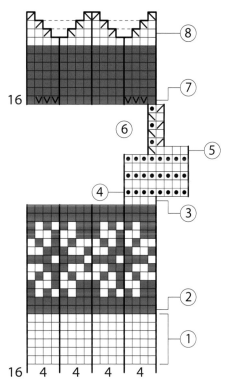

Mini Socks with Flowers

STRIPED FLAG MINI SOCKS

Knit a string of sock flags. Our socks display the flag colors of the five Nordic countries, but you can use the colors of any national flag you want. All the socks are strung along a cord.

SKILL LEVEL
Intermediate

MATERIALS
Yarn:
Small amounts of fine wool yarn good for felting. I used CYCA #1 (fingering), Finull PT2 from Rauma Ullvarefabrikk (100% pure new wool, 191 yd/175 m / 50 g) and CYCA #2 (sport, baby), Tove from Sandnes (100% wool, 175 yd/ 160 m / 50 g). It's important to match the stripe colors as closely as possible to the flag colors of each country, if you want the socks to look right.
Needles: U. S. size 1.5 or 2.5 / 2.5 or 3 mm: Set of 5 dpn.
Notions: A cord to string the flags onto for hanging.

Instructions

① CO 16 sts over 1 dpn. Work from the chart for your chosen flag. Knit 4 rows (2 ridges) back and forth. The rows begin at center back.

② Now divide the sts evenly over 4 dpn and join to work in the round. Continue following the charted pattern, working the leg to the heel in St st and stranded color knitting.

③ The heel is worked back and forth in St st. Knit the first 4 sts.

④ Turn and purl back over the next 8 sts. Leave rem sts on needle or holder for instep. Work 5 rows in St st over the 8 heel flap sts.

⑤ **Rnd 6:** K4, ssk; turn.

⑥ Continue as follows for heel turn:
WS: Sl 1 purlwise, p2tog.
RS: Sl 1 knitwise, ssk.
Rep WS and RS rows until 2 sts rem on heel.

⑦ Now continue in the round. The rnd begins at the center of the sole.
Rnd 1: K1 of heel; pick up and knit 3 sts on side of flap; k8 across instep; pick up and knit 3 sts on opposite side of flap, k1 of heel. Now work the foot as shown on the chart.

⑧ Shape the toe at each side on every rnd as shown on the chart. Cut yarn and draw end through 4 rem sts.

FINISHING

Seam garter st cuff at center back. Weave in all ends neatly on WS. Felt socks (see page 18). Stretch socks into finished shape, lay flat, and leave until completely dry.

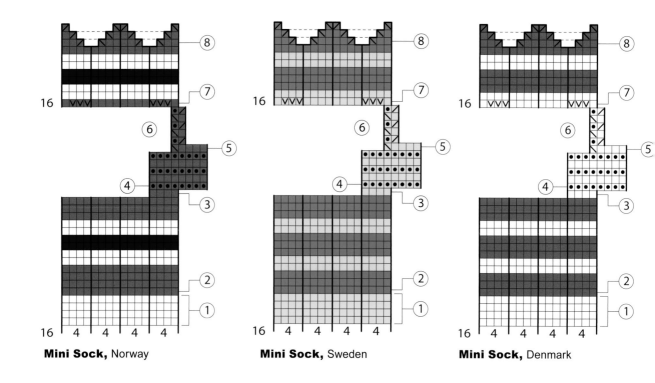

Mini Sock, Norway

Mini Sock, Sweden

Mini Sock, Denmark

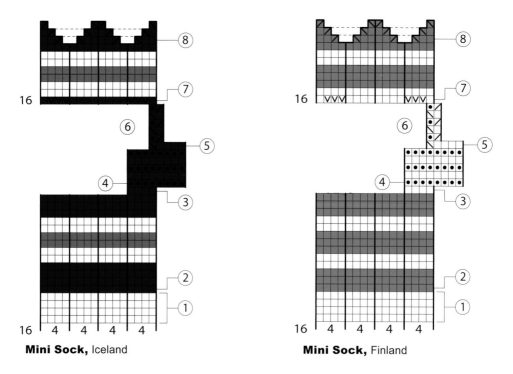

Mini Sock, Iceland

Mini Sock, Finland

INITIALED MINI SOCKS

Make a friend happy with a pair of mini socks bearing their initials. Initialed socks for every person in my family hang on our Christmas tree!

SKILL LEVEL
Experienced

MATERIALS
Yarn:
Small amounts of fine wool yarn good for felting. I used CYCA #1 (fingering) Finull PT2 from Rauma Ullvarefabrikk (100% pure new wool, 191 yd/175 m / 50 g) and CYCA #2 (sport, baby) Tove from Sandnes (100% wool, 175 yd/ 160 m / 50 g). Each of the designs uses white as the contrast color and for the cuffs, heels, and toes.
Needles: U. S. size 1.5 or 2.5 / 2.5 or 3 mm: Set of 5 dpn.
Notions: Cords for hanging the socks on the tree.

Instructions

① With White, CO 16 sts over 1 dpn. Work from the Mini Sock chart. Knit 4 rows (2 ridges) back and forth. The rows begin at center back. Now divide the sts evenly over 4 dpn and join to work in the round. Change to MC and knit 2 rnds.

② Continue, following the charted pattern with the initials you want. Knit 2 rnds with MC.

③ The heel is worked back and forth in stockinette. Knit the first 4 sts.

④ Turn and purl back over the next 8 sts. Leave rem sts on needle or holder for instep. Work 5 rows in stockinette over the 8 heel flap sts.

⑤ **Rnd 6:** K4, ssk; turn.

⑥ Continue as follows for heel turn:
WS: Sl 1 purlwise, p2tog.
RS: Sl 1 knitwise, ssk.
Rep WS and RS rows until 2 sts rem on heel.

⑦ Now continue in the round. The rnd begins at the center of the sole.
Rnd 1: K1 of heel; pick up and knit 3 sts on side of flap; k8 across instep; pick up and knit 3 sts on opposite side of flap, k1 of heel. Now work the foot as shown on the chart.

⑧ Shape the toe at each side on every rnd as shown on the chart. Cut yarn and draw end through 4 rem sts.

FINISHING

Seam garter st cuff at center back. Weave in all ends neatly on WS. Felt socks (see page 18). Stretch socks into finished shape, lay flat, and leave until completely dry.

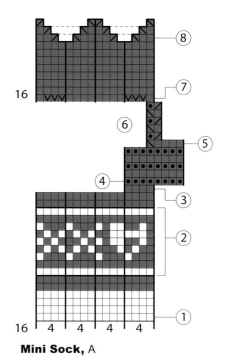

Mini Sock, A

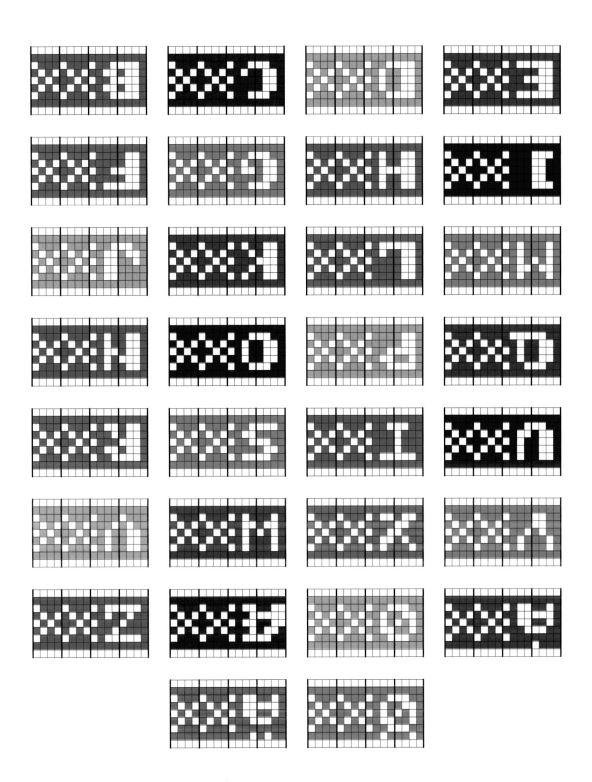

STRIPED MINI STOCKINGS

Striped long stockings for the elf mother, She wears these all winter.

SKILL LEVEL
Intermediate

MATERIALS
Yarn:
Small amounts of fine wool yarn good for felting. I used CYCA #1 (fingering) Finull PT2 from Rauma Ullvarefabrikk (100% pure new wool, 191 yd/175 m / 50 g). Colors:
White, Red, and Green.
Needles: U. S. size 1.5 or 2.5 / 2.5 or 3 mm: Set of 5 dpn.
Notions: Cords for hanging the socks on the tree; decorative charms.

Instructions

① With White, CO 16 sts over 1 dpn. Divide the sts evenly over 4 dpn and join to work in the round. Work from the *Striped Mini Stocking* chart. Work 3 rnds k1, p1 ribbing as shown on the chart and then knit 1 rnd.

② Continue in charted stripe pattern.

③ The heel is worked back and forth in stockinette. With Green, knit the first 4 sts.

④ Turn and purl back over the next 8 sts. Leave rem sts on needle or holder for instep. Work 5 rows in stockinette over the 8 heel flap sts.

⑤ **Rnd 6:** K4, ssk; turn.

⑥ Continue as follows for heel turn:
WS: Sl 1 purlwise, p2tog.
RS: Sl 1 knitwise, ssk.
Rep WS and RS rows until 2 sts rem on heel.

⑦ Now continue in the round. The rnd begins at the center of the sole.
Rnd 1: K1 of heel; pick up and knit 3 sts on side of flap; k8 across instep; pick up and knit 3 sts on opposite side of flap, k1 of heel. Now work the foot as shown on the chart.

⑧ Shape the toe at each side on every rnd as shown on the chart.

FINISHING
Cut yarn and draw end through 4 rem sts. Weave in all ends neatly on WS. Felt socks (see page 18). Stretch socks into finished shape, lay flat, and leave until completely dry.

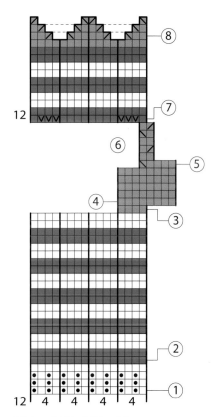

Striped Mini Stockings

FINE ACCESSORIES
FOR CHRISTMAS

Some items are so "Christmas" that they almost
can't be used any other time of the year. Other
things work just as well before or after Christmas,
for every day or for parties. In this section, you'll
find patterns for small garments and decorations in
traditional colors that say Christmas, but you could
just as easily make them with other colors and use
them any time of year.

BOWS

Decorate the children, your beloved, the potted plants, your cuddly pets, shoes, or the Christmas tree with a fine bow for Christmas. Everything will be enhanced! With a bow, a common bottle or pot can be transformed into a fun Christmas decoration, the "everyday" dress into a Christmas dress, in the blink of an eye!

These bows are worked in the round. Afterwards, the ends are folded in toward each other at the center back and seamed. Finish by knitting a little band to attach around the center of the bow.

SKILL LEVEL
Experienced

MATERIALS
Yarn:
CYCA #1 (fingering) Søstrene Grene Anna & Clara (100% cotton, 175 yd/ 160 m / 50 g).
Yarn Amounts and Colors:
One ball of each color will be enough for several bows.
Substitute Yarn: Yarn for a gauge of 28-30 stitches in 4 in / 10 cm will make bows of about the same size.
Needles: U. S. size 1.5 / 2.5 mm: Set of 5 dpn.

GAUGE
28-30 sts = 4 in / 10 cm.
Adjust needle size to obtain correct gauge if necessary

POLKA DOT BOW

Instructions

With Red, CO 28 sts. Divide sts evenly over 4 dpn and join to work in the round. Knit 21 rnds for half of the back of the bow.

Now work from the *Polka Dot Bow* chart. Work the first pattern repeat (A) 4 times and then complete the pattern with the last row of dots for a total of 44 pattern rnds. Cut white yarn. Knit 21 rnds with Red for the second half of the back. BO.

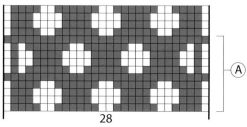

Polka Dot Bow

BOW WITH DIAGONAL STRIPES

Instructions

With Light Blue, CO 28 sts. Divide sts evenly over 4 dpn and join to work in the round. Knit 23 rnds for half of the back of the bow.

Now work from the *Bow with Diagonal Stripes* chart. Repeat the charted rows until there are a total of 48 pattern rnds. Cut White yarn. Knit 23 rnds with Light Blue for the second half of the back. BO

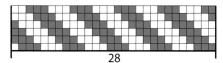

Bow with Diagonal Stripes

STRIPED BOW

Instructions

With Red, CO 28 sts. Divide sts evenly over 4 dpn and join to work in the round. Knit 22 rnds for half of the back of the bow.

Now work in stripe pattern: *Knit 2 rnds with White; knit 2 rnds with Red*; rep * to * until there are a total of 12 White stripes. Cut White. Knit 22 rnds with Red for the second half of the back. BO.

FINISHING FOR ALL BOWS
Knit the little band back and forth in seed st, alternating knit and purl sts. After 1st rnd, work purl over knit and knit over purl. With MC, CO 7 sts. Knit 1 rnd. Continue, following the Band chart. BO. Carefully steam press the bow so it flattens, making sure the pattern remains symmetrical and the beginning of the rnd is centered underneath. Sew the ends together to make a ring. Place the seed-st band around the bow at the middle and sew it to the bow on the back.

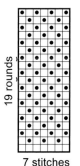

Band

WINTER BIRDS

Some birds fly south once winter begins setting in here in Norway. However, the bullfinches and magpies are among those birds who stay put. Both birds are easy to recognize and spot in the winter landscape. Bullfinches stand out vividly against all that white and gray with their red breasts, and the black and white magpies spread happiness with their adorable hopping and bouncing.

We people are also happy to be out in the snow and cold, but not without cozy hats, mittens, socks, and sweaters. Here are a few patterns for those garments with winter birds pictured in the patterning. The perfect Christmas gifts for everyone, big or small!

CHILDREN'S HAT WITH BULLFINCHES

Knit an especially elaborate hat to keep little ones cozy. Four bullfinches at the front of the hat fit perfectly into the pattern, and come forth completely with finishing when the black and gray colors of the feathers are embroidered in.

At the edge, the hat has a folded-in facing, which makes the hat sit in place well to keep the ears warm.

SKILL LEVEL
Experienced

SIZE
Approx. 2-4 years

FINISHED MEASUREMENTS
Circumference: Approx. 19¾ in / 50 cm
Length: 8¼ in / 21 cm

MATERIALS
Yarn: CYCA #1 (fingering) Rauma Baby Panda (100% Merino wool, 191 yd/175 m / 50 g).

Yarn Amounts and Colors:
Approx. 15 g (not including pompom) White 11
Approx. 20 g Gray 12
Approx. 10 g Red 18
Approx. 2 g Green 78
Approx. 2 g Brown-black 110 (same color as for the magpies in the next pattern)
Substitute Yarn: CYCA #1 (fingering) baby wool yarn for a gauge of 30 stitches in 4 in / 10 cm on U. S. size 1.5 / 2.5 mm needles.
Needles: U. S. sizes 0 and 1.5 / 2 and 2.5 mm: 16 in / 40 cm circulars; set of 5 dpn
U. S. size 1.5 / 2.5 mm for the crown.
Notions: Tapestry needle for embroidering feather colors.

GAUGE
32 sts in pattern on larger needles = 4 in / 10 cm.
Adjust needle sizes to obtain correct gauge if necessary.

Instructions

① With Red and smaller circular, CO 140 sts. Join, being careful not to twist cast-on row; pm for beginning of rnd. Work following *Chart 1, Hat*, repeating the pattern around. The rnd begins at center back of the hat. Work the facing by repeating the first row of the chart 7 times. After completing the facing, knit 1 rnd with White.

② Work the eyelet rnd as the foldline for the facing. After completing eyelet rnd, change to larger circular. The pattern repeat is 14 sts which are repeated 10 times per rnd. Pm on every 14th st to make counting easier. Work to end of Chart 1.

③ Now work following *Chart 2, Hat*. Pattern A = 14 sts and is repeated 3 times. Pattern B = 28 sts and is worked 2 times. Pattern C = 14 sts and is repeated 3 times.

④ After completing border panel, continue with the snowflake pattern. Each snowflake consists of 1 White knit st on the 1st rnd and then p1 in White over the previous knit st.

⑤ Rep the snowflake pattern until there are a total of 5 snowflake tiers.

Crown shaping: Place 4 markers around with 35 sts between each marker. Change to dpn when sts no longer fit around circular. Continue the snowflake pattern throughout crown.

Decrease on every other rnd as follows: *Ssk, knit until 3 sts before next marker, k2tog, k1*; rep * to * around (= 4 rep total).

Decrease the same way 2 times, knitting 2 rnds between each decrease rnd. Now, decrease on every rnd. When 12 sts rem, cut yarn and draw end through rem sts; tighten.

FINISHING

Fold facing to inside and sew down with loose stitches. Embroider the bullfinch feather colors (*Chart 3, Bullfinches, duplicate stitch*) with duplicate st. Weave in all ends neatly on WS. Make a pompom and attach securely to top of hat.

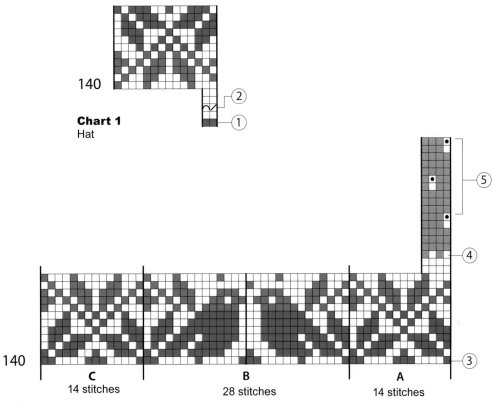

Chart 1
Hat

140

Chart 2
Hat

140

C
14 stitches

B
28 stitches

A
14 stitches

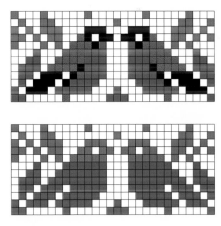

Chart 3
Bullfinches, duplicate stitch

SWEATER WITH WINTER BIRDS

No doubt the Christmas feeling will be spread with such a delightful sweater decorated with bullfinches and magpies. The sweater is knitted with a fine baby wool and the bullfinches on the front are embroidered after the knitting is complete. This is a somewhat long model that will fit for a long time. The top and bottom of the body have folded-in facings. The boat neck guarantees that the child's head will fit into the sweater without getting stuck.

SKILL LEVEL
Experienced

SIZE
Approx. 2-4 years

FINISHED MEASUREMENTS
Chest Circumference: Approx. 27½ in / 70 cm
Total Length: 13¾ in / 35 cm
Inner Sleeve Length: 9½ in / 24 cm
Sleeve Circumference: at top: 11¾ in / 30 cm; at cuff: 6 in / 15 cm

MATERIALS
Yarn: CYCA #1 (fingering) Rauma Baby Panda (100% Merino wool, 191 yd/175 m / 50 g).
Yarn Amounts and Colors:
Approx. 64 g White 11
Approx. 110 g Gray 12
Approx. 10 g Red 18
Approx. 13 g Green 78
Approx. 5 g Brown-black 110
Substitute Yarn: CYCA #1 (fingering) baby wool yarn for a gauge of 30 stitches in 4 in / 10 cm on U. S. size 1.5 / 2.5 mm needles.
Needles: U. S. sizes 0 and 1.5 / 2 and 2.5 mm: 24-32 in / 60-80 cm circulars; set of 5 dpn U. S. size 1.5 / 2.5 mm for the sleeves.
Notions: Tapestry needle for embroidering feather colors.

GAUGE
32 sts in pattern on larger needles = 4 in / 10 cm.
Adjust needle size to obtain correct gauge if necessary.

Instructions

The sweater is worked in the round, from the bottom up. The armholes are cut open after knitting the sides.

BODY
① With Gray and smaller circular, CO 224 sts. Join, being careful not to twist cast-on row; pm for beginning of rnd. The rnds begin at the side with the front being worked first. Work following *Chart 1, Sweater.* Begin with knitting 7 rnds for the facing.

② Work the eyelet rnd as the foldline for the facing. After completing eyelet rnd, change to larger circular. Continue following the chart. The repeat with the magpies is worked over 28 sts, repeated 8 times around, so pm every 28 sts to make counting easier.

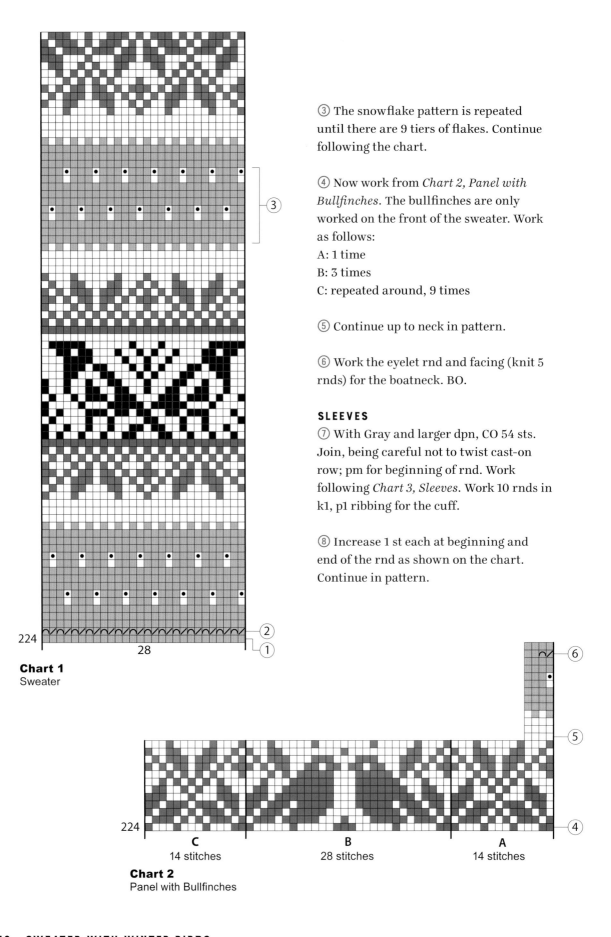

③ The snowflake pattern is repeated until there are 9 tiers of flakes. Continue following the chart.

④ Now work from *Chart 2, Panel with Bullfinches*. The bullfinches are only worked on the front of the sweater. Work as follows:
A: 1 time
B: 3 times
C: repeated around, 9 times

⑤ Continue up to neck in pattern.

⑥ Work the eyelet rnd and facing (knit 5 rnds) for the boatneck. BO.

SLEEVES
⑦ With Gray and larger dpn, CO 54 sts. Join, being careful not to twist cast-on row; pm for beginning of rnd. Work following *Chart 3, Sleeves*. Work 10 rnds in k1, p1 ribbing for the cuff.

⑧ Increase 1 st each at beginning and end of the rnd as shown on the chart. Continue in pattern.

Chart 1
Sweater

224
28

Chart 2
Panel with Bullfinches

224

C
14 stitches

B
28 stitches

A
14 stitches

⑨ Increase on every 5th rnd as indicated on the chart until sleeve is complete. The increases are always made in the first snowflake rnd. Continue as est until sleeve is 9 in / 23 cm long. Work 1 pattern repeat with 3 rnds Gray and then a rnd alternating k1 White, k1 Gray. Cut Gray. Work 6 rnds in stockinette with White for the panel at the top of the sleeve and then the facing which will be sewn down on the WS.

Make the second sleeve the same way.

FINISHING

Armholes: Measure the width of the sleeve top. Measure the same length down the side from the shoulder "seam." Baste down the center side stitch to mark the placement and depth of the armhole. Machine-stitch 2 lines on each side of the basting line. Carefully cut armhole open down basting line. Gently steam press the garment under a damp pressing cloth.

Press under the foldlines for the facings at top and bottom. Sew down facings to WS with loose stitches. Seam shoulders.

Attach sleeves: Turn body inside out. Lightly steam press sleeves and then set them inside the body with RS of sleeve facing RS of body. Make sure the beginning of the rnd turns down over so it's on the underside of the sleeve. Pin-baste and then attach sleeves with mattress stitch. The seam should go through the first rnd of the facing on the sleeve. Lightly steam press, and then sew the facings to the sleeves inside the body with loose stitches.

Use Gray and Black yarn to embroider the feathers on the bullfinches. Weave in all ends neatly on WS.

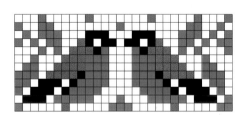

Bullfinches, Duplicate Stitch Guide

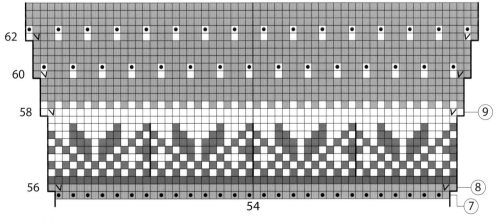

Chart 3
Sleeves

BULLFINCH MITTENS

By the time this book was printed, hundreds of pairs of bullfinch mittens had already been knitted. Maybe you'd also like to knit a pair? Here's the history behind the Bullfinch mittens:

On Facebook, you'll find the "Jorid Linvik Design" group, which is, of course, moderated by yours truly. For Advent 2017, I designed a pair of mystery knit-along mittens for the group. Mittens were knitted north and south and the pattern was discussed back and forth in the group. Many were very curious about what the design would look like, all the way until the last bit of the puzzle was shared and the bullfinches saw the light of day.

Since these bullfinches were already so popular, I let them fly onto hats, sweaters, socks, Christmas stockings, and potholders. Maybe they'll land on a knitted garment near you...

SKILL LEVEL
Experienced

SIZE
Women's (Men's)

MATERIALS
Yarn: CYCA #3 (DK, light worsted) Du Store Alpakka Sterk (40% Merino wool, 40% alpaca, 20% nylon, 150 yd/137 m / 50 g).
Yarn Amounts and Colors:
50 g (might need a 2nd ball for Men's size) White or Natural White
50 g Gray or Dark Gray
Approx. 25 g Red
Small amount of Black to embroider wings.
Substitute Yarn: Yarn with the same gauge recommendations as for Sterk.
Needles: U. S. sizes 1.5-2.5 / 2.5-3 mm (U. S. 2.5-4 / 3-3.5 mm): Set of 5 dpn.
Notions: Tapestry needle for embroidering feather colors.

GAUGE
25 (23) sts in pattern on gauge size needles = 4 in / 10 cm.
Adjust needle size to obtain correct gauge if necessary.

Instructions

① With White, CO 50 sts. Divide the sts as evenly as possible onto 4 dpn and join to work in the round. Begin with *Chart 1, Cuff*. The pattern is worked in the round. The first 5 rnds are the facing, which will be turned under and sewn down once the mittens are finished.

② **Eyelet rnd:** Work following chart. After working eyelet rnd, continue to end of chart; cut Red.

③ Now work following *Chart 2, Left Mitten* or *Chart 3, Right Mitten*. Divide the sts over the dpn as indicated on bottom of chart.

④ **Shape thumb gusset:** On every other rnd, increase 2 sts as shown on the chart. After completing increases, there are 60 sts around.

⑤ **Thumbhole:** With a smooth contrast color yarn, knit the 12 sts marked with the heavy red line on the chart for the thumbhole. Slide the sts back to left needle and knit in pattern.

⑥ After completing thumbhole, work both mittens the same way, following *Chart 4, Right and Left Mitten*.

⑦ Shape top, decreasing at each side as shown on the chart.

⑧ Decrease 1 extra st at each side as shown on chart.

⑨ With white and Kitchener st, join the front and back sets of sts.

⑩ **Thumb:** Insert a dpn into the sts below scrap yarn at thumbhole and another dpn into sts above scrap yarn. Carefully remove scrap yarn = 12 + 12 sts. Work following *Chart 5, Left Thumb* or *Chart 6, Right Thumb* and, on the first rnd, increase to 26 sts by picking up and knitting 1 st at each side as indicated on the chart.

⑪ Begin top shaping.

⑫ Cut yarns and draw ends through rem sts; tighten.

FINISHING

Use duplicate st to embroider the black and red feathers on the body of each bird (see *Chart 7*). Weave in all ends neatly on WS. When you knit the second mitten, make sure the thumb is on the opposite side from the thumb on the first mitten.

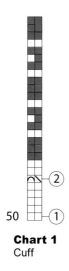

Chart 1
Cuff

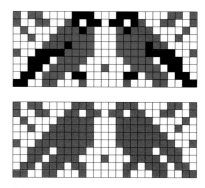

Chart 7
Bullfinches, Duplicate Stitch Guide

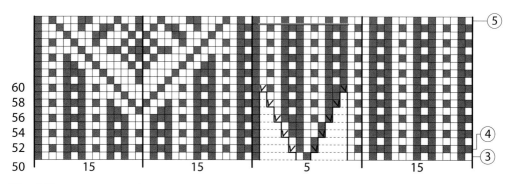

Chart 2
Left Mitten

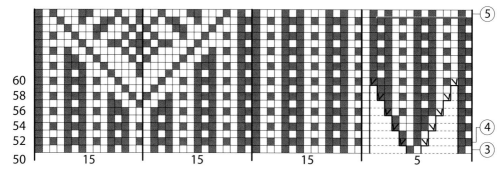

Chart 3
Right Mitten

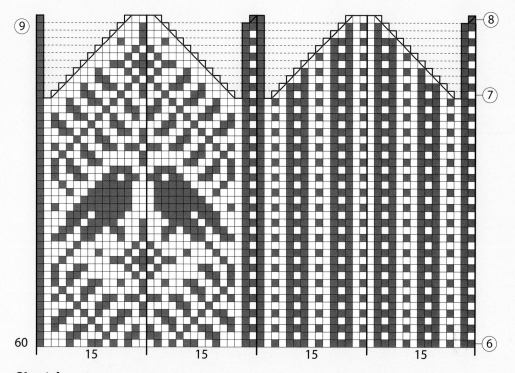

Chart 4
Right and Left Mitten

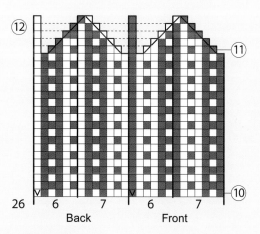

Chart 5
Left Thumb

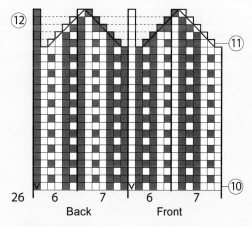

Chart 6
Right Thumb

WINTER BIRD SOCKS

The magpies have scarfed up all the food from the feeder and now they're keeping an eye out from the top of the spruce tree. Magpies aren't as welcome in gardens as bullfinches, but as a sock motif both birds are equally good. These socks feature the so-called "Russian heel" where both the heel and foot are worked with two strands to make the socks especially sturdy and warm.

DESCRIPTION AND CONSTRUCTION METHODS FOR RUSSIAN SOCKS

The entire sock is knitted in the round, including the heel. The sock is knitted straight from the cuff to the toe. The only thing you have to remember is to knit in a strand of smooth contrast color scrap yarn where the heel will be knitted in later.

When the scrap yarn is removed later, it will leave a large opening. The heel is knitted around this opening. After 2 rounds, the heel is shaped at the sides as for the toe.

The placement for this scrap yarn is marked with a heavy horizontal line on the chart. Find a length of leftover yarn that contrasts strongly with the working yarn so you can see it clearly after you knit it in. This yarn is only a "holding" thread in the knitting.

Knit until you are beginning the first stitch above the heavy line. Drop the working yarn and use the scrap yarn to knit over the 37 stitches marked by the heavy line. Cut the scrap yarn, leaving enough of a tail on each end so it won't pull out of the stitches. Push both ends of the scrap yarn to the wrong side. Slide the scrap yarn stitches back to the left needle.

Now pick up the working yarn and work in pattern across the scrap yarn as if nothing had happened.

Finish knitting the sock and fasten off.

Heel: Insert double-pointed needles into the stitches below and above the scrap yarn and carefully remove the scrap yarn so you don't drop any stitches. Once the scrap yarn is removed, there will be a hole where the heel will be worked around. Half of the stitches (on the sole) will be upside down when the scrap yarn is removed. Make sure that these stitches sit correctly on the needle as for knit stitches so your work will be as neat and even as possible.

Begin at the side and knit the stitches for the underside of the foot (sole)—these stitches are upside down in relation to the new round. Check the chart and your stitches to make sure the stitch counts match. See the numbers below the Heel chart to double check. Knit the heel in the round, shaping it at each side as shown on the chart.

It's likely that there will be a little hole at each side of the heel in the transition between the leg and sole. Tighten these holes with the yarn ends when you weave in the ends.

SIZE
Women's (Men's)

MATERIALS
Yarn: CYCA #3 (DK, light worsted) Du Store
Alpakka Sterk (40% Merino wool, 40% alpaca,
20% nylon, 150 yd/137 m / 50 g).
Yarn Amounts and Colors:
50 g (might need a 2nd ball for Men's size)
White or Natural White 50 g Gray or Dark
Gray Approx. 25 g or less Red
Small amount of Black to embroider wings.

Substitute Yarn: CYCA #3 (DK, light worsted)
for a gauge of 24 stitches in 4 in / 10 cm on
U. S. size 2.5 / 3 mm needles.
Needles: U. S. sizes 2.5-4 / 3-3.5 mm (smaller
size recommended for Women's socks and
larger size for Men's): Set of 5 dpn.
Notions: Tapestry needle for embroidering
feather colors.

GAUGE
25 (23) sts in pattern on gauge size needles =
4 in / 10 cm.
Adjust needle size to obtain correct gauge if
necessary.

Instructions

① With Gray, CO 68 sts. Divide the sts evenly
over 4 dpn and join to work in the round.
Work following *Chart 1, Foot,* beginning with
k2, p2 ribbing.

② Increase 4 sts spaced as indicated on chart
= total of 72 sts. Divide the sts on the 4 dpn
as shown by numbers below chart. Work in
pattern until the magpie panel is complete.

③ Decrease 2 sts as shown on chart = 70 sts
rem.

④ **Heel opening:** With a smooth, contrast
color scrap yarn, knit the 37 heel sts marked
by the heavy red line on the chart. The heel
will be worked here later. Now continue in
pattern after the 1st st of the rnd (where the
scrap yarn sts start).

⑤ Shape the foot at each side as indicated on
the chart = a total of 3 decrease rnds.

⑥ Begin toe shaping: decrease 2 sts at each
side on every rnd.

⑦ **Last rnd:** Decrease 1 extra st at each side.

⑧ Join the rem 7 sts of instep with the 7 sts
on sole with gray yarn and Kitchener st.

⑨ **Heel:** The heel begins at the sole. Carefully
remove scrap yarn (see page 147) = 37 + 37
sts. Work following *Chart 2, Heel,* and, on the
first rnd, pick up and knit 1 st at each side as
indicated on chart.

⑩ After 2 rnds, begin shaping at the sides as
for the toe.

⑪ Decrease 2 extra sts on last rnd.

⑫ Join the sets of heel sts as for the toe.

FINISHING
Use duplicate st to embroider the black and
red feathers on the bullfinches. Weave in
all ends neatly on WS. Make the 2nd sock the
same way.

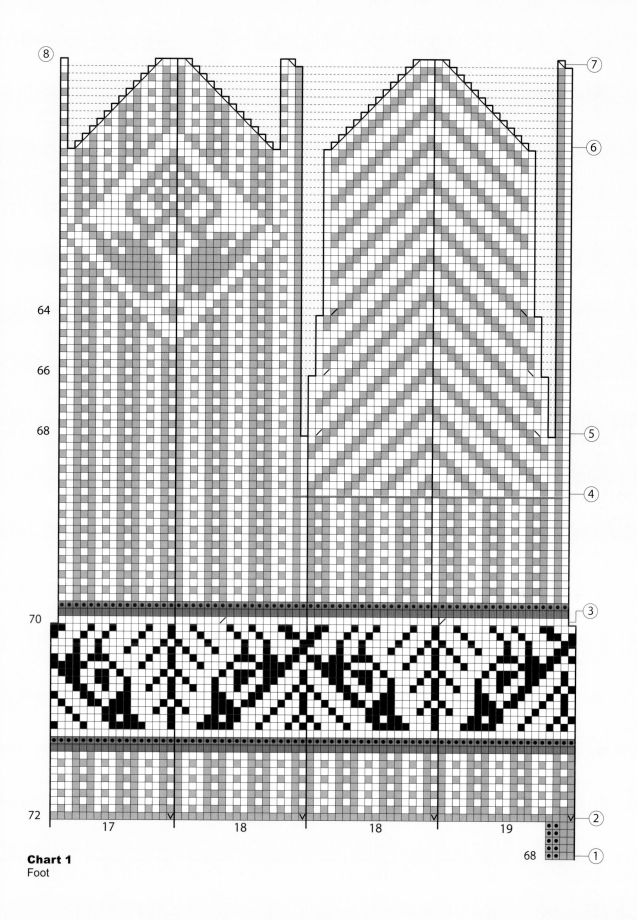

Chart 1
Foot

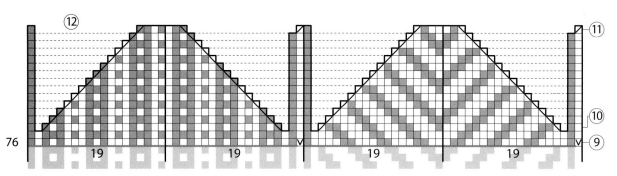

Chart 2
Heel

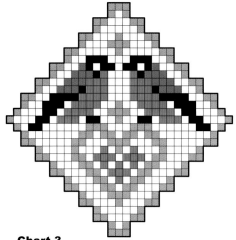

Chart 3
Bullfinches, Duplicate Stitch Guide

HAT WITH MAGPIES

Funny magpies are a good entertainment when they fly between spruce tree tops. Even though this hat has fewer stitches than the children's hat with bullfinches, it is larger and will fit up to a man's size.

SKILL LEVEL
Experienced

SIZE
Women's (Men's)

MATERIALS
Yarn: CYCA #3 (DK, light worsted) Du Store Alpakka Sterk (40% Merino wool, 40% alpaca, 20% nylon, 150 yd/137 m / 50 g).

Yarn Amounts and Colors:
50 g White or Natural White
50 g Gray or Dark Gray
Approx. 15 g Black
Small amount of Christmas Red
Substitute Yarn: CYCA #3 (DK, light worsted) for a gauge of 24 stitches in 4 in / 10 cm on U. S. size 2.5 / 3 mm needles.
Needles: U. S. sizes 2.5 or 4 / 3 or 3.5 mm (smaller size recommended for Women's socks and larger size for Men's): 16 in / 40 cm circular and set of 5 dpn.

GAUGE
25 (23) sts in pattern on smaller (larger) size needles = 4 in / 10 cm. Adjust needle size to obtain correct gauge if necessary.

Instructions

① With Gray and circular needle, CO 120 sts. Join, being careful not to twist cast-on row. Pm for beginning of rnd. Work following the *Hat* chart. The pattern repeats around and the hat begins with 7 rnds of k2, p2 ribbing.

② Increase 6 sts evenly spaced around = (k20, M1) around = 126 sts.

③ Increase 1 st at the beginning of the rnd and 1 st at middle for a total of 128 sts. Now work the magpie panel. The panel has 32 sts per repeat and is worked 4 times around. Pm after every 32nd st.

④ Decrease 1 st each at beginning and middle of rnd = 126 sts rem.

⑤ **Crown shaping:** Decrease as shown on the chart. When the sts no longer fit around circular, change to dpn. Work the charted decreases and pattern around to end of chart. Cut yarn and draw end through rem sts; tighten.

FINISHING

Weave in all ends neatly on WS. Make a plump pompom and securely attach it to top of hat.

Hat

128

126

120

126

1

2

3

4

5

THE ELF MOTHER'S HEART

For my Facebook group's Advent knit-along project in 2016, I designed a pair of mittens with an elf motif. The knit-along participants only got one section of the pattern at a time, but here you can have the whole pattern all at once!

These mittens with their dancing elves have been extremely popular, and many have requested the pattern on a matching hat and socks. So I adapted the heart and Christmas tree motifs from the mittens and placed those motifs on both. The entire series is called "The Elf Mother's Heart."

THE ELF MOTHER'S HEART-MITTENS

Why not go dancing at Christmas time? It sets the mood, and the surly elves on the mitten tops look like they need a little encouragement.

The same pattern can be knitted for both women and men. If you chose a wool yarn, the mittens can be gently felted after knitting. These mittens were knitted with Rauma's Finullgarn on needles U. S. size 1.5 / 2.5 mm and then carefully felted. Both mittens are knitted the same way except for the thumb placement.

SKILL LEVEL
Experienced

MATERIALS

For Women's Mittens: Choose a yarn recommended for 26-27 sts in 4 in / 10 cm with needles U. S. size 1.5 or 2.5 / 2.5-3 mm: set of 5 dpn.

For Men's Mittens: Choose a yarn to be worked at 22-23 sts in 4 in / 10 cm with needles U. S. size 2.5 / 3 mm: set of 5 dpn.

Yarn:

CYCA #1 (fingering) Finull PT2 from Rauma Ullvarefabrikk (100% pure new wool, 191 yd/175 m / 50 g).

Yarn Amounts and Colors:

One ball each Red and White for a pair of mittens. Use a small amount of Blue or Brown for the eyes and for the thumb scrap yarn.

Instructions

① With Red, CO 56 sts. Divide sts evenly over 4 dpn and join to work in the round. Begin with *Chart 1, Cuff*, repeating the pattern around.

② On the first rnd after the ribbing, increase 1 st after the 1st st on each dpn = 60 sts total. Continue following the charted pattern. Some of the stitches are purled, and the round with the eyes uses either blue or brown for the eyes.

③ Eyelet round for cord.

④ Continue to *Chart 2, Mitten Hand*.

⑤ **Thumbhole:** Knit the marked 11 sts for thumbhole with smooth, contrast color scrap yarn. The left mitten thumb sts are on needle 1 while those for the right hand are on needle 2. Push the ends of the scrap yarn to the WS. Slide scrap yarn sts to left needle and continue in pattern.

⑥ Begin top shaping: Decrease at each side as shown on the chart. There is an extra decrease at the tip.

⑦ With White yarn and Kitchener st, join the front and back sets of stitches.

⑧ **Thumb:** Insert a dpn into row below scrap yarn and another dpn into row above scrap yarn. Carefully remove the

scrap yarn = 11 + 11 sts. Work following *Chart 3, Right Thumb* or *Chart 4, Left Thumb*.

Rnd 1: Increase to a total of 25 sts by picking up and knitting sts as indicated on the chart.

Work 19 rnds in pattern and then shape top. You might want to pm for beginning of rnd as it can be difficult to see which st it is at this point.

⑨ **Shape top:** On the first decrease rnd, there are only 3 decreases; this is to ensure there will be the same number of sts on each side of the thumb.

⑩ Cut yarn and draw ends through the 6 rem sts; tighten.

FINISHING
Weave in all ends neatly on WS. Make the second mitten the same way but don't forget to position the thumb on the correct side.

Chart 1
Cuff

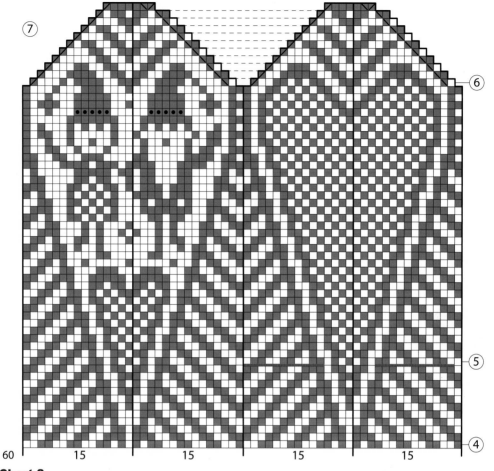

Chart 2
Mitten Hand

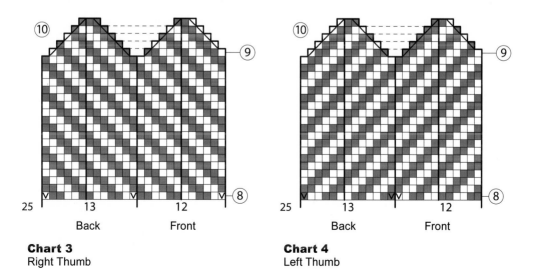

Chart 3
Right Thumb

Chart 4
Left Thumb

THE ELF MOTHER'S HEART-SOCKS

The hearts here were copied from the mittens and adapted for socks. Combined with the diagonal lines, these socks will be as great for Christmas as for the rest of the year.

The socks shown in the photo were knitted with Sisu from Sandnes Garn on needles U. S. size 2.5 / 3 mm. They are a women's medium to fit shoe sizes U. S. 5½-8½ / Euro 36-39. The same pattern can be used for either women's or men's sizes.

SKILL LEVEL
Experienced

MATERIALS
For Women's Socks: (shoe sizes U. S. 5½-8½ / Euro 36-39) Sock yarn recommended for gauge of 26-27 sts in 4 in / 10 cm. 1 ball of each color. Needles sizes U. S. 1.5-2.5 / 2.5-3 mm: set of 5 dpn.
For Men's Socks: (shoe sizes U. S. 7-11 / Euro 40-44) Sock yarn recommended for gauge of 22-24 sts in 4 in / 10 cm. 1 ball of each color. Needles sizes U. S. 2.5-4 / 3-3.5 mm: set of 5 dpn.
Yarn: CYCA #1 (sock/fingering/baby) Sandnes Garn Sisu (80% wool, 20% nylon; 191 yd/ 175 m / 50 g)

Instructions

With Red, CO 64 sts. Divide sts evenly over 4 dpn and join to work in the round. Work 9 rnds in k1, p1 ribbing and then knit 1 rnd, purl 1 rnd.

① Work following *Chart 1, Sock Leg*. Divide the sts on the needles as noted at the bottom of the chart. On the first rnd, increase 1 st on each needle = 68 sts as shown on the chart. The rnds begin at center back.

② Now decrease 4 sts as indicated on the chart = 64 sts rem. Complete charted rows and cut yarn.

③ Work following *Chart 2, Heel*. The heel is worked back and forth over the 33 center back sts. Place rem sts on a holder for the instep. With Red, begin 16 sts from beginning of rnd. Work 33 sts.

④ Turn work and k1, p1 across.

⑤ Continue working back and forth with knit over knit and purl over purl until there are a total of 26 rows in heel flap.

⑥ **Heel turn:** Knit until 13 sts rem on needle, ssk. Turn work and purl back. The rem heel sts rem on needle but will be gradually decreased away one by one with the center sts.

⑦ Rep these two rows until 11 sts rem:
WS: P10, p2tog; turn.
RS: Sl 1 purlwise, k9, ssk; turn.

⑧ Continue with *Chart 3, Foot*:
With Red, pick up and knit 16 sts along left side of heel flap, k11 centered on heel, pick up and knit 16 sts along other side of heel. With both colors, work the 31 sts across instep. Make sure that the pattern matches that on the sock leg.

⑨ Decrease 1 st at each side of heel on every other rnd as shown on chart. Complete charted rows.

⑩ Now work from *Chart 4, Foot and Toe*.

⑪ **Toe:** As shown on chart, decrease on each side on every other row. Work k1, p1 ribbing on the instep—on alternate rows as shown on chart.

⑫ When 26 sts rem, begin decreasing on every rnd.

⑬ When 10 sts rem, join the two sets of sts with Kitchener st. Weave in all ends neatly on WS. Make second sock the same way.

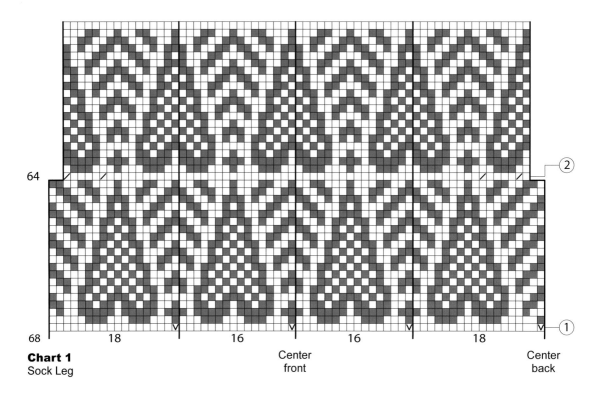

Chart 1
Sock Leg

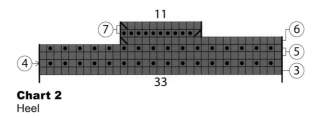

Chart 2
Heel

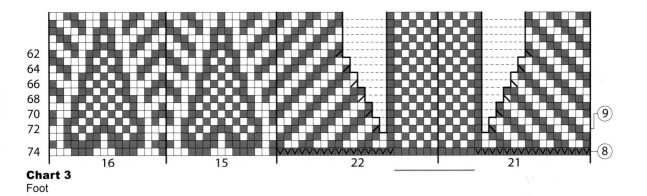

Chart 3
Foot

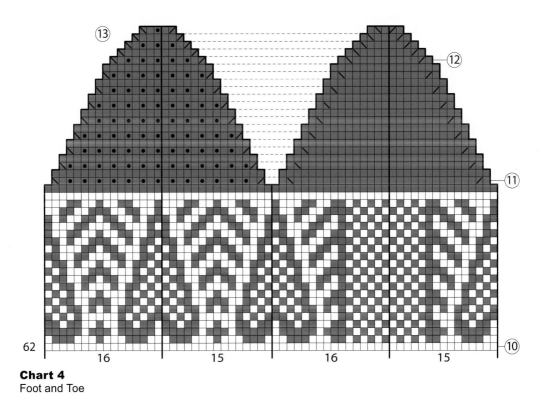

Chart 4
Foot and Toe

THE ELF MOTHER'S HEART– HAT

The Elf Mother's heart pattern works perfectly on a hat because the width and length of this pattern are the same. This is a nice cozy hat you can knit for yourself or for someone you care about.

The hat can be knitted in either women's or men's sizes from the same pattern—just use different needle sizes. I decorated my hat with a faux fur pompom I bought, but you can make a pompom yourself, or leave it off entirely.

SKILL LEVEL
Experienced

MATERIALS
For Women's Hat: Yarn recommended for gauge of 22-24 sts in 4 in / 10 cm. 1 ball of each color. Needles U. S. size 4 / 3.5 mm: 16 in / 40 cm circular and set of 5 dpn.

For Men's Hat: Yarn recommended for gauge of 22-24 sts in 4 in / 10 cm. 1 ball of each color. Needles U. S. size 6 / 4 mm: 16 in / 40 cm circular and set of 5 dpn.

Yarn: The hat shown here was knitted with CYCA #3 (DK, light worsted) Du Store Alpakka Sterk (40% Merino wool, (40% alpaca, 20% nylon, 150 yd/ 137 m / 50 g) on needles U. S. size 4 / 3.5 mm.

Instructions

① With White and circular, CO 120 sts. Join, being careful not to twist cast-on row. Pm for beginning of rnd. Work following the *Hat* chart, repeating the motifs around. Begin with k2, p2 ribbing for 12 rnds.

② (K15, M1) 8 times around = 128 sts. Continue following the chart to crown shaping.

③ **Crown shaping:** Decrease as shown on chart. When the sts no longer fit around circular, change to dpn.

④ (K2tog) around. Cut yarn and draw end through rem sts; tighten. Weave in all ends neatly on WS.

128

Chart
Hat

120

WARMING CHRISTMAS GIFTS

A very important aspect of Christmas is, of course,
presents. For those of us who knit, producing
Christmas presents can be a double pleasure.
Instead of getting stressed as we go around the
shops before Christmas, we can lean back in
a comfy chair with some knitting to enjoy.
Everything we knit has a personal touch, and the
recipients can easily see their gifts were made with
both time and effort.

Many of the items previously shown in the book
make good Christmas gifts. Now you'll find some
patterns for fine garments that warm—in several
ways—and can be worn all winter.

GOOD OLD-FASHIONED CHRISTMAS GIFTS

In the old days, it was common to make Christmas presents. Most often these were necessary and useful items. Children and adults received new mittens, socks, and hats to replace the old worn-out gifts from the previous year. It was important that the garments be of the best possible quality so they'd last to the next Christmas without needing to be patched and darned along the way.

DURABLE SOCKS

These are socks for active people and a basic for the wardrobe. Previously this type of sock was worn inside boots or as an inner sock on cold winter days. For anyone participating in outdoor activities, it's important to take along a good pair of wool socks because cold weather can come on suddenly and expectedly even in summer.

Knitted in gray heather yarn, these socks take on an authentic, traditional look that's simultaneously rustic and beautiful. You might also choose to knit them in other colors, or with stripes.

The pattern is for socks in 3 different sizes: women's, men's, and children's. You can easily adjust the length of the leg or foot.

SKILL LEVEL
Intermediate

MATERIALS
Yarn: CYCA #2 (sport, baby) Viking of Norway Sportsragg (60% wool, 20% nylon, 20% acrylic, 109 yd/100 m / 50 g).
Yarn Amount and Color:
150 g for Men's, 100 g for Women's, and 50-100 g for Children's: Light Gray Heather.
Substitute Yarn:
Strong sock yarn with the same gauge as for Sportsragg.
Needles: U. S. size 2.5 / 3 mm: Set of 5 dpn.

GAUGE
23-24 sts = 4 in / 10 cm.
Adjust needle size to obtain correct gauge if necessary.

Instructions

Sizes: Men's (Women's, Children's)

CO 56 (48, 44) sts. Divide sts evenly onto 4 dpn and join to work in the round. Work around in k2, p2 ribbing for 8 (6, 4¾) in / 20 (15, 12) cm.

Heel flap: Place the 30 (26, 22) sts at center front on a holder for instep while you work the heel. Arrange the sts so that there are 2 purl sts at each side of the instep sts.

The heel is worked back and forth over the 26 (22, 22) sts at center back. Increase 2 sts at center back on the 1st row = 28 (24, 24) sts.

Work 22 (18, 16) rows back and forth in St st.

Heel turn: Begin on RS of heel flap. Knit until 9 (8, 6) sts rem, ssk. Turn and purl back. The rem heel sts will gradually be decreased with center sts on every row.

Rep these two rows until 12 (10, 10) sts rem:

WS: P11 (9, 9), p2tog; turn.
RS: K11, 9, 9), ssk; turn.

Foot: Cut yarn and begin at the left side of the heel. Pick up and knit 10 (9, 8) sts along heel flap, k12 (10, 8) across heel, pick up and knit 10 (9, 8) sts on other side of flap.

Work in k2, p2 ribbing across the 30 (26, 22) instep sts (the ribbing continues up to toe shaping).

On the 4th and 7th rnds after the heel turn, decrease as follows: Knit until 2 sts rem before the first 2 purl sts of instep, k2tog. Knit the 2 sts after the 2 last instep purl sts, ssk. For Men's and Women's sizes: Rep only one time after 6 new rnds. Continue until the foot measures 6¾ (6, 4¾) in / 17 (15, 12) cm from the heel or measure against a sock that fits well. The toe shaping begins right after the tip of the little toe.

Toe shaping: Work around in St st only. Divide the sts on the dpn so that the instep and sole each have the same number of sts (divided over 2 dpn for each side). Decrease on every other rnd at each side: K1, ssk, knit until 3 sts rem on opposite side, k2tog, k1.

When 7 sts rem on each needle, decrease as est on every rnd. When 10 or 12 sts total rem, cut yarn. Join rem sets of sts with Kitchener st. Weave in all ends neatly on WS. Make the second sock the same way.

WORK MITTENS

For anyone who does a lot of chores out in the cold, these pretty mittens are a Christmas gift of love. The mittens are excellent to wear when skiing, carrying wood, shoveling snow, or carrying out any other outdoor activities. In extreme cold, these mittens can line larger mittens for double the warmth.

Both mittens are knitted the same way and will fit well on the hands for sports and work. Use them alternately on the right and left hands for even wear. These mittens are knitted tightly and then felted to fit the wearer's hands for size and firmness.

The same pattern can be used to make mittens in several sizes. Knit the mittens somewhat larger than the needed measurements and then felt them down to size.

SKILL LEVEL
Intermediate

SIZES
Men's (Women's, Children's)

MATERIALS
The mittens shown here were knitted with:
Yarn: CYCA #3 (DK, light worsted), House of Yarn Linde Garn Ren Ull (100% wool, 109 yd/100 m / 50 g) or a similar weight wool that can be felted.
Needles: U. S. size 6-7 / 4-4.5 mm (U. S. 6 / 4 mm, U. S. 2.5 / 3 mm): set of 5 dpn.
GAUGE
20-22 (22-23, 26-27) sts = 4 in / 10 cm. Adjust needle size to obtain correct gauge if necessary.

Instructions

① With MC (Green), CO 40 sts. Divide sts onto 4 dpn and join to work in the round. Work following *Chart 1, Work Mitten*. Begin with k2, 2 ribbing for approx. 23 rnds in stripe sequence: 5 rnds MC, (2 rnds CC, 4 rnds MC) 3 times. Cut CC.

② Knit 1 rnd and arrange sts with 10 sts on each of the 4 dpn.

③ Now increase 2 sts on every 3rd rnd as shown on the chart. Continue shaping until there are a total of 56 sts around.

④ Knit 2 rnds after last increase rnd. Add extra rnds if necessary for a long hand.

⑤ **Thumbhole:** K20, place the next 16 sts on a holder. CO 2 new sts over the gap (marked with a V on the chart) and then k20 to end of rnd. Knit 20 rnds to tip of little finger.

⑥ **Shaping at little finger:** Decrease 1 st each at the beginning and end of rnd as shown on the chart. Decrease the same way once more (see chart).

⑦ Now begin decreasing 2 sts at each side on every rnd to top of chart.

⑧ Cut yarn and draw end through rem sts; tighten.

⑨ **Thumb:** *Chart 2, Work Mitten, Thumb.* Place the 16 sts set aside for thumb onto dpn.
Rnd 1: Knit around, picking up and knitting 1 st each at beginning and end of rnd = 18 sts total.

⑩ Decrease 1 st each at beginning and end of rnd = 16 sts rem.

⑪ Knit 2 rnds and then decrease as shown on chart. Knit 6 rnds.

⑫ Decrease 1 st each at beginning and end of rnd = 14 sts rem. Knit 3 rnds.

⑬ (K2tog) around. Cut yarn and draw end through rem sts; tighten.

Make the second mitten the same way.

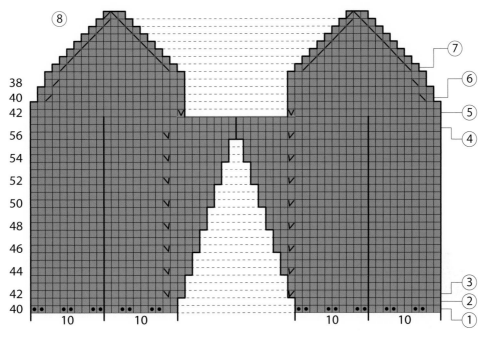

Chart 1
Work Mitten

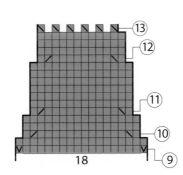

Chart 2
Work Mitten, Thumb

EVERYDAY HATS

Most days of the year are ordinary days with "normal" weather—no extremes of cold or heat. On those days, you just need an everyday hat knitted "straight up." Choose one or two colors that suit the recipient of the hat. Neutral colors will complement every outfit.

The hats in the photo were knitted with Sterk from Du Store Alpakka. Excluding the pompom, each hat took just 50 g of yarn. The yellow hat was knitted in white and yellow, while the purple hat is striped with white for a garter stitch brim.

SKILL LEVEL
Intermediate

MATERIALS
Yarn: Yarn recommended for a gauge of 21-22 sts in 4 in / 10 cm. The circumference of the hat is approx. 19 ¾ in / 50 cm. The garter stitch brim makes the hat very elastic, so it'll fit a range of head sizes. You'll need about 50 g of yarn + some extra for a pompom—or buy a ready-made faux fur pompom.
Needles: U. S. size 4 / 3.5 mm: 16 in / 40 cm circular and set of 5 dpn.

Instructions

With circular and MC, CO 102 sts. Work back and forth in striped garter stitch: (Knit 2 rows MC, 2 rows CC) until there are a total of 11 ridges. Now join to knit in the round; pm for beginning of rnd. Increase 3 sts evenly spaced around = 105 sts. Alternate colors every rnd or continue in only one color. Knit 44 rnds or until hat is 7 in / 18 cm long.

Crown shaping:
Decrease Rnd 1: (K5, k2tog) around.
Knit 4 rnds.
Change to dpn when sts no longer fit around circular.

Decrease Rnd 2: (K4, k2tog) around.
Knit 3 rnds.
Decrease Rnd 3: (K3, k2tog) around.
Knit 2 rnds.
Decrease Rnd 4: (K2, k2tog) around.
Knit 1 rnd.
Decrease Rnd 5: (K2tog) around.
Knit 2 rnds.

FINISHING
Cut yarn and draw end through rem sts; tighten. Seam garter-stitch brim. Weave in all ends neatly on WS.

THE
SOFTEST
PACKAGES

Some packages are so delicate that the paper tears even when it's barely touched—packages holding things like, for example, a hat, headband, or mittens that were knitted in lovely soft wool and then felted.

If you're mailing gifts like these through the post office, it's a good idea to pack them in a box so the mail carrier won't accidentally poke holes in the paper along the way.

FELTED MITTENS

These mittens are long and delightful. They warm the hands up to the arms and right through to the heart. The mittens have wide cuffs and will stay in place well when pulled over sweater sleeves.

Both mittens are knitted the same way except for the thumb placement.

SKILL LEVEL
Intermediate

SIZES
Men's (Women's)

MATERIALS
Yarn: CYCA #2 (sport, baby) Tove from Sandnes (100% wool, 175 yd/160 m / 50 g).
Yarn Amounts and Colors:
50 g each Dark Blue and White for one pair of mittens.
Needles: U. S. size 6 / 4 mm (U. S. 4 / 3.5 mm): Set of 5 dpn.

The mittens are knitted large and then felted to desired finished size. See page 18 for more on felting.

Instructions

① With Blue (MC), CO 48 sts. Divide the sts evenly onto 4 dpn = 12 sts per needle. Join to work in the round; pm at beginning of rnd. Work following *Chart 1, Right and Left Mittens.* Begin with 3 rnds k1, p1 ribbing.

② **Thumbhole:** With a smooth contrast color yarn, k9 of the marked sts. Left mitten: heavy white line; right mitten: heavy red line. Slide the sts back to left needle and work in pattern.

③ Begin top shaping.

④ After completing charted rows, cut yarn and draw end through rem sts; tighten.

⑤ **Thumb:** Insert a dpn through sts of row below scrap yarn and another dpn in row above scrap yarn. Carefully remove scrap yarn = 9 + 9 sts. Work from *Chart 2, Thumb.*

Rnd 1: Increase to 20 sts by picking up and knitting 1 st at each side as shown on the chart.

⑥ Shape top as shown on chart.

⑦ Cut yarn and draw end through rem sts; tighten.

FINISHING
Weave in all ends neatly on WS. Knit the second mitten as for first, adjusting placement of thumbhole. Felt mittens to size (see page 18).

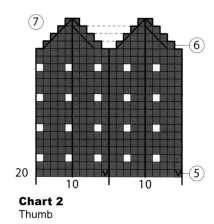

Chart 2
Thumb

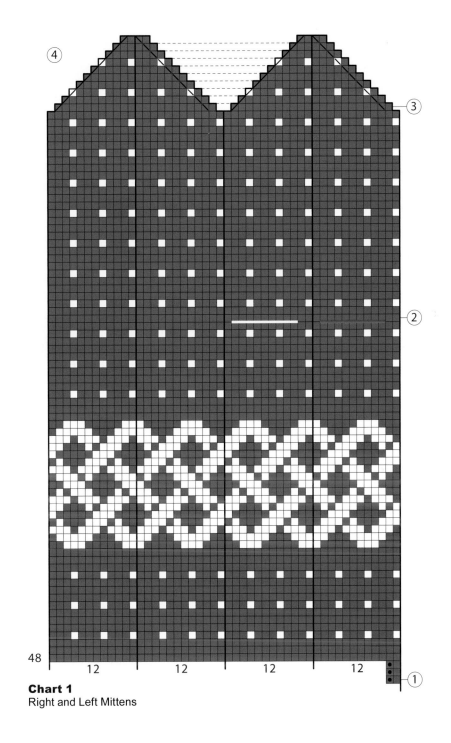

④

③

②

48

12 12 12 12

①

Chart 1
Right and Left Mittens

CHILDREN'S FELTED MITTENS

Soft mittens for little children's hands. The long cuffs can be pulled over jacket sleeves, but will also stay in place well if the mittens are put on before the jacket.

These mittens are quick and easy to knit. The newly knitted mittens will actually fit an adult hand, but then they're felted down to a child's size.

Both mittens are knitted the same way except for the thumb placement.

SKILL LEVEL
Experienced

SIZES
Child 2-4 years (4-8 years)

MATERIALS
Yarn: CYCA #2 (sport, baby), Tove from Sandnes (100% wool, 175 yd/160 m / 50 g).
Yarn Amounts and Colors:
50 g each Beige and Brown for one pair of mittens.
Needles: U. S. size 4 / 3.5 mm (U. S. 6 / 4 mm): Set of 5 dpn.

The mittens are knitted large and then felted to desired finished size. See page 18 for more on felting.

Instructions

① With Beige (MC), CO 40 sts. Divide the sts evenly onto 4 dpn = 10 sts per needle. Join to work in the round; pm at beginning of rnd. Work following *Chart 1, Right and Left Mittens*. Begin with 3 rnds k2, p2 ribbing.

② **Thumbhole:** With a smooth contrast color yarn, k7 of the marked sts. Right mitten: heavy red line; left mitten: heavy blue line. Slide the sts back to left needle and work in pattern.

③ Begin top shaping.

④ After completing charted rows, cut yarn and draw end through 8 rem sts; tighten.

⑤ **Thumb:** Insert a dpn through sts of row below scrap yarn and another dpn in row above scrap yarn. Carefully remove scrap yarn = 7 + 7 sts. Work from *Chart 2, Thumb.*
Rnd 1: Increase to 16 sts by picking up and knitting 1 st at each side as shown on the chart.

⑥ Shape top as shown on chart.

⑦ Cut yarn and draw end through 4 rem sts; tighten.

FINISHING
Weave in all ends neatly on WS. Knit the second mitten as for the first, adjusting placement of thumbhole. Felt mittens to size (see page 18).

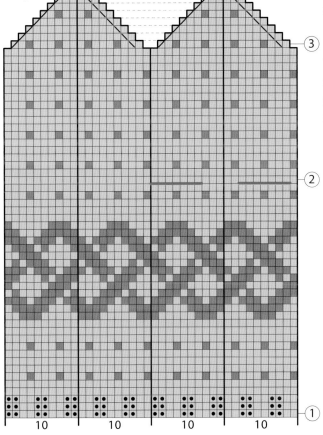

Chart 1
Right and Left Mittens

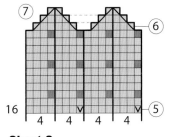

Chart 2
Thumb

FELTED HAT AND HEADBAND

The same pattern as for the mittens appears here on a hat and headband set, but in a somewhat wider variation. These soft accessories for the head are felted and fit well around the ears without scratching.

SKILL LEVEL
Experienced

SIZES
Child (Adult)
The pieces are knitted large and then felted to size. You can decide if you want a long or short hat. The short hat covers the ears while the long version is slouchy.

MATERIALS
Yarn: CYCA #2 (sport, baby) Tove from Sandnes (100% wool, 175 yd/160 m / 50 g).
Yarn Amounts and Colors:
50 g each Beige and Brown will make a hat (long or short), or 1-2 headbands.
Needles: U. S. size 6-7 / 4-4.5 mm: 16 in / 40 cm circular + set of 5 dpn.
Notions: Add a pompom to the hat if you want!

Instructions

① With MC and circular, CO 88 (96) sts. Join, being careful not to twist cast-on row; pm for beginning of rnd. Work following the *Hat and Headband* chart. The pattern repeats around.

② Increase 8 sts evenly spaced around = total of 96 (104) sts. Continue in pattern. **Headband:** Work up to the chart row marked Headband. Knit 1 rnd, at the same time, decreasing 8 sts evenly spaced around = 88 sts rem. Work 4 rnds k2, p2 ribbing and then BO loosely. **Short Hat:** Knit to the chart row marked Short Hat and then skip up to crown shaping.

③ **Crown shaping:** Decrease as indicated on the chart. When sts no longer fit around circular, change to dpn. After completing charted rows, cut yarn. Draw end though rem sts; tighten. Weave in all ends neatly on WS.

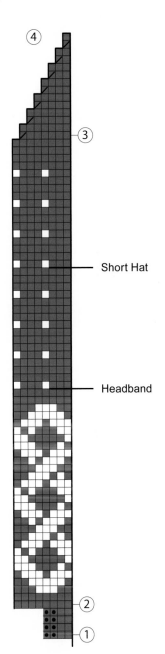

④

③

— Short Hat

— Headband

②

①

Hat and Headband

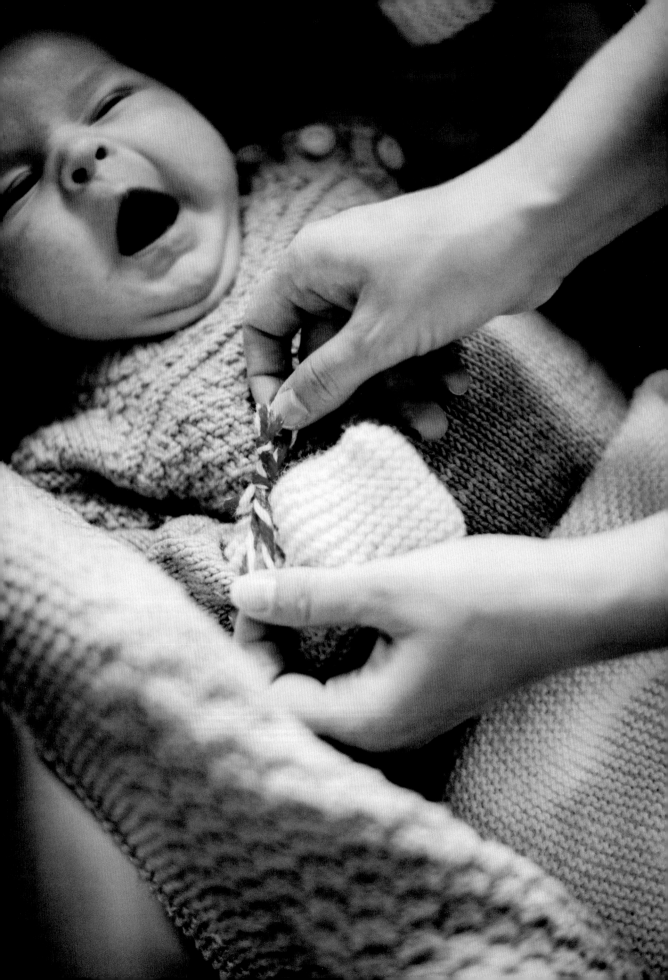

LAST BUT NOT LEAST

You can knit a few quick gifts right up to Christmas
Eve, even if time is short.

Maybe you have a little yarn stash at home? One
ball of yarn can become a pair of slippers, a hat,
wrist warmers, or a cowl. Surprise a colleague
at work with a gift on the last work day before
Christmas, or make someone you know happy with
an unexpected present.

WOMEN'S SLIPPERS WITH RIDGES AND POMPOMS

These easy-to-work ridged slippers are a natural Christmas gift—or you can make them to be used by Christmas guests with cold feet. If the slippers are to be a gift, knit them in colors that the recipient will appreciate. These slippers are striped but, of course, you make them in one color if you prefer.

If you've knitted slippers before, you can use your own judgment and add or subtract rows to make the precise length needed or you can add or subtract from the number of stitches in width for the desired height. These slippers are quite elastic and can be worn by many different size feet.

SKILL LEVEL
Intermediate

SIZE
To fit women's shoe sizes approx. U. S. 5½-9½ / Euro 36-40

MATERIALS
Yarn: CYCA #3 (DK, light worsted), Du Store Alpakka Sterk (40% Merino wool, 40% alpaca, 20% nylon, 150 yd/137 m / 50 g).
Yarn Amounts and Colors:
20 g Red
20 g Dark Red
Small amounts White and Black for the edgings and pompoms
Needles: U. S. sizes 2.5-4 / 3-3.5 mm: Circular or 2 long straight needles.

GAUGE
20 sts in pattern = 4 in / 10 cm.
Adjust needle size to obtain correct gauge if necessary.

Instructions

These slippers are worked back and forth in garter stitch throughout (2 knit rows = 1 garter ridge). If you are knitting with 2 colors, change colors every 2 rows/rnds. Begin at the back of the slipper and work forward. The slipper is finished by folding it along the center of the sole and then joining the front and back.

Ridge 1: With Red, CO 34 sts. Knit 1 row.

WS: K16, (M1, k1) 4 times, M1, k15 = 40 sts.

Knit 60 rows = 30 ridges.

Ridge 31: Decrease 6 sts at center of front: K14, (k2tog) 6 times, k14.

Knit 1 row and then BO.

FINISHING
Fold the slipper in half and then neatly seam the front.
Edging: The edge is worked back and forth over all the sts. With RS facing, beginning at center back, pick up and knit sts along the edge all the way around. Turn work and knit back. Knit 1 ridge for the edging, but, on the second row of this ridge, (k2tog) 6 times at center front.
Seam the slipper at center back. Make the second slipper the same way.

QUICK MEN'S SLIPPERS WITH "SHOE STRINGS"

Some men think it isn't cool to go around wearing slippers embellished with pompoms or tassels. These easily knit slippers, however, have fake shoe strings sewn on for a more masculine look. The strings help the slippers look more like shoes.

SKILL LEVEL
Intermediate

SIZE
To fit men's shoe sizes approx. U. S. 6½-11 / Euro 36-40.

MATERIALS
Yarn: CYCA #2 (sport, baby) Viking of Norway Sportsragg (60% wool, 20% nylon, 20% acrylic, 109 yd/100 m / 50 g).

Yarn Amount and Color:
65 g Blue; use a fine, black yarn for the shoe strings.
Substitute Yarn:
Strong sock yarn with the same gauge as for Sportsragg, about 23 sts in 4 in / 10 cm.
Needles: U. S. size 2.5-4 / 3-3.5 mm: Set of 5 dpn.
Notions: 4 beads for the ends of shoe strings.

GAUGE
Approx. 23 sts on needles U. S. 4 / 3.5 mm = 4 in / 10 cm.
Adjust needle size to obtain correct gauge if necessary.

Instructions

CO 34 sts. Work following the *Men's Slipper* chart. The first part of the slipper is worked back and forth.

① Knit 1 row.

② **WS:** K15, (M1, k1) 5 times, M1, k14 = 40 sts.

③ Continue knitting back and forth in garter st until there are a total of 24 ridges.

④ Divide the sts over 4 dpn with 10 sts on each needle. The rest of the slipper is worked in the round. Begin with a rnd of purl sts. On every other rnd, work 1 knit st more (with 1 less purl st) on each side as shown on the chart until the first and last 10 sts of rnd are knit.

⑤ **Toe shaping:** Decrease at each side on every other rnd as indicated on chart.

⑥ BO rem sts. Seam the top side of the slipper to the sole using mattress st.

FINISHING

Seam the slipper at center back. Weave in all ends neatly on WS. Make the second slipper the same way.

Shoe strings: Braid or twist the strings with fine yarn. Sew the strings to the slippers so they will look as if they are threaded for shoes. Sew a bead to the end of each string.

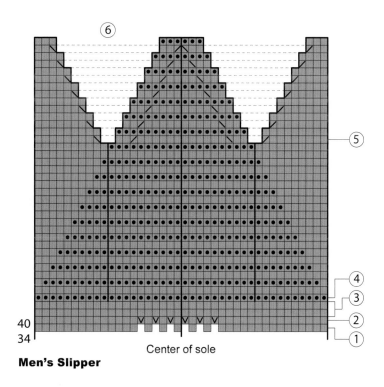

40
34

Center of sole

Men's Slipper

QUICK WOMEN'S SLIPPERS

The smooth shaping of the slippers in the previous pattern can, of course, suit a woman's foot. The women's version omits the shoe strings but there are many other options for embellishing these slippers according to your personal taste. You can knit them in various colors and decorate them with silk ribbon, pompoms, bows ... or even edge the top with fringe! I enhanced my slippers with red pompoms.

If you've knitted slippers before, you can use your own judgment and add or subtract rows to make the precise length needed; or you can add or subtract from the number of stitches in width for the desired height.

SKILL LEVEL
Intermediate

SIZE
To fit women's shoe sizes approx. U. S. 5½-8 / Euro 36-38.

MATERIALS
Yarn: CYCA #2 (sport, baby) Viking of Norway Sportsragg (60% wool, 20% nylon, 20% acrylic, 109 yd/100 m / 50 g).
Yarn Amount and Color:
50 g White and small amount of Red for the pompoms.
Substitute Yarn:
Strong sock yarn with the same gauge as for Sportsragg, about 23 sts in 4 in / 10 cm.
Needles: U. S. size 2.5-4 / 3-3.5 mm: Set of 5 dpn.

GAUGE
Approx. 23 sts on needles U. S. 4 / 3.5 mm = 4 in / 10 cm.
Adjust needle size to obtain correct gauge if necessary.

Instructions

CO 30 sts. Work following the *Women's Slipper* chart. The first part of the slipper is worked back and forth.

① Knit 1 row.

② **WS:** K13, (M1, k1) 5 times, M1, k12 = 36 sts.

③ Continue knitting back and forth in garter st until there are a total of 20 ridges.

④ Divide the sts over 4 dpn with 9 sts on each needle. The rest of the slipper is worked in the round. Begin with a rnd of

purl sts. On every other rnd, work 1 knit st more (with 1 less purl st) on each side as shown on the chart until the first and last 9 sts of rnd are knit.

⑤ **Toe shaping:** Decrease at each side on every other rnd as indicated on chart.

⑥ BO rem sts. Seam the top side of the slipper to the sole using mattress st.

FINISHING

Seam the slipper at center back. Weave in all ends neatly on WS. Make the second slipper the same way.

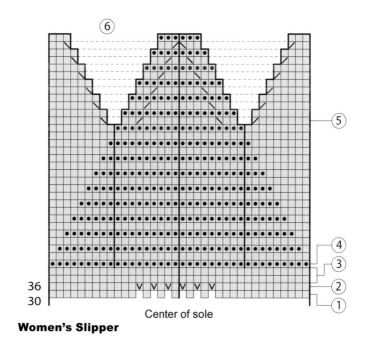

Women's Slipper

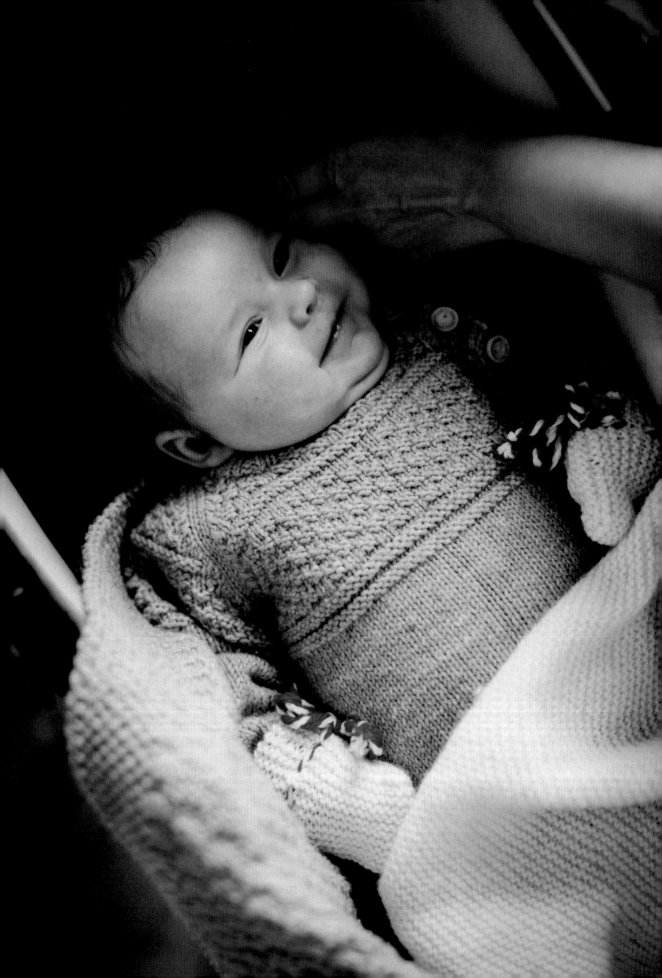

QUICK BABY SLIPPERS AND MITTENS WITH TIES

For anyone who, say, likes to take a little nap in the baby carriage, a pair of soft slippers and small mittens is an excellent way to keep the fingers and toes toasty and warm. These slippers and mittens are simply shaped and held in place with ties. The baby slippers are knitted the same way as for the larger slippers in the previous patterns, but these have an extra folded edge with an eyelet row to thread the ties through.

SKILL LEVEL
Intermediate

SIZE
Baby, 0-6 months

MATERIALS
Yarn: CYCA #3 (DK, light worsted) Du Store Alpakka Sterk (40% Merino wool, 40% alpaca, 20% nylon, 150 yd/137 m / 50 g).
Yarn Amount and Color:
50 g White for both slippers and mittens.
Substitute Yarn: Yarn with the same gauge recommendations as for Sterk, approx. 23 sts in 4 in / 10 cm.
Needles: U. S. sizes 2.5-4 (3-3.5) mm: Set of 5 dpn.
Notions: You can twist or braid the cords, preferably with several colors, for the mittens and slippers. Or buy some cords—just double-check the length, and trim them if necessary.

GAUGE
23 sts in pattern = 4 in / 10 cm.
Adjust needle size to obtain correct gauge if necessary.

Instructions

Begin at back of heel and knit back and forth all along the opening. Later, the work is joined and the second half of the slipper is knitted in the round. If you've knitted slippers before, you can use your own judgment and add or subtract rows to make the precise length needed; or you can add or subtract from the number of stitches in width for the desired height.

CO 34 sts. Work following the *Baby Slipper* chart.

① Knit 1 row.

② **WS:** K15, (M1, k1) 5 times, M1, k14 = 40 sts.

③ **Eyelet row:** K8, yo, k2tog, k20, k2tog, yo, k8. Rep the eyelet row 3 times with 5 knit rows between each eyelet row (see chart).

④ BO the first 8 sts of the row.

⑤ BO the first 8 sts of the row; purl over next 24 sts. Divide the sts onto 3 dpn with 8 sts on each needle; join to work in the round. As indicated on the chart, on every other rnd, knit 1 st more (with 1 less purl st) at each side.

⑥ **Toe shaping:** On every other rnd, decrease at each side as shown on the chart.

⑦ Cut yarn and draw end through rem 8 sts; tighten.

FINISHING
Seam the slipper at center back. Weave in all ends neatly on WS. Insert cord through eyelet row. Make the second slipper the same way.

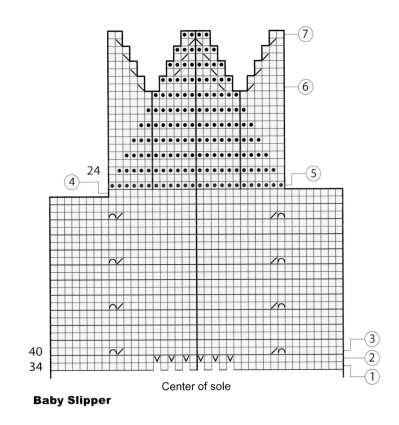

Center of sole

Baby Slipper

Instructions

Knit these mittens back and forth in garter stitch and then fold them for seaming at the sides.

① CO 38 sts and work following the *Baby Mitten* chart. Begin by knitting 1 row.

② **WS:** K16, (M1, k1) 5 times, M1, k17 = 44 sts.

③ **Eyelet row:** *K7, yo, k2tog, k26, k2tog, yo, k7. Knit 5 rows*. Rep from * to * 3 more times (see chart).

④ **Last row:** K16, (k2tog) 6 times, k16 = 38 sts rem.

FINISHING

BO. Fold mitten in half down the center. Seam both sides. Insert cord through eyelet row. Make the second mitten the same way.

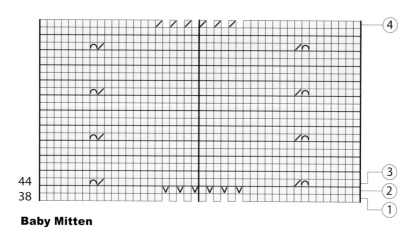

Baby Mitten

FRINGED COWL

This pretty cowl stays in place quite nicely and keeps you warm where you need it most—around the neck and chest. Paired with the wrist warmers in the next pattern, it spiffs up any outfit!

Feel free to knit this cowl in whatever yarn you want that doesn't prickle or scratch. Use needles 1-2 sizes larger than recommended on the ball band.

The cowl is worked back and forth, folded in half for a double triangle and then seamed at the back. The two short sides of the triangle are embellished with a thick row of fringe. The cowl pulls on over the head.

BLUE COWL

SKILL LEVEL
Intermediate

FINISHED MEASUREMENTS
13¾ in / 35 cm for a short cowl to fit child or adult.

MATERIALS
Yarn: CYCA #1 (fingering) Viking Nordlys from Gjestdal (75% superwash wool, 25% nylon, 383 yd /350 m / 100 g.
Yarn Amount and Color:
Approx. 35 g including fringe: Blue.
Needles: U. S. size 6 / 4 mm: circular.

RED COWL

SKILL LEVEL
Intermediate

FINISHED MEASUREMENTS
15¾ in / 40 cm for a long cowl to fit adult.

MATERIALS
Yarn:
Cowl: CYCA #6 (super bulky) Du Store Alpakka Pus (70% alpaca, 17% acrylic, 13% nylon, 109 yd /100 m / 50 g.
Fringe: fine baby yarn.
Yarn Amount and Color:
Approx. 50 g for cowl: Dark Red
Approx. 20 g for fringe: Dark Brown.
Needles: U. S. size 10½-11 / 7 mm: circular.

Instructions

With circular, CO 6 sts. Working back and forth, knit 2 rows (= 1 ridge). Pm after 3rd st. Continue as follows:
Knit to marker, sl m to right needle, yo, knit to end of row.
The piece gradually becomes a square. Continue knitting as est until piece measures approx. 13 in / 35 cm for a child or 15¾ in / 40 cm for an adult. BO.

FINISHING
Fold the cowl and seam it at the back.

FRINGE
Wrap the yarn evenly around a template for desired length. Cut open wraps at one end. Working with pairs of strands for baby yarn or one strand for heavier yarn, attach a fringe between each ridge along cowl edges with a crochet hook.

WRIST WARMERS WITH BUTTONS AND FRINGE

These fun wrist warmers are probably the easiest items you can knit. Use any yarn you like with needles 1-2 sizes larger than recommended on the ball band. The wrist warmers are loosely knitted to make them elastic and soft. The cuffs shown here use the same yarns as for the cowls.

You can knit wrist warmers in any size you want, just cast on and knit back and forth until the piece fits around your wrist. Embellish them with beads, buttons, pompoms, or whatever else you like—or just leave them elegantly simple.

BLUE WRIST WARMERS
SKILL LEVEL
Beginner

MATERIALS
Yarn: CYCA #1 (fingering), Viking Nordlys from Gjestdal (75% superwash wool, 25% nylon, 383 yd /350 m / 100 g.
Yarn Amount and Color:
Approx. 20 g (including fringe) Blue.
Needles: U. S. size 6 / 4 mm: circular.
Notions, optional: decorative button(s).

RED WRIST WARMERS
SKILL LEVEL
Beginner

MATERIALS
Yarn:
CYCA #6 (super bulky), Du Store Alpakka Pus (70% alpaca, 17% acrylic, 13% nylon, 109 yd /100 m / 50 g.
Fringe: fine baby yarn.
Yarn Amount and Color:
Approx. 15 g Dark Red
Small amount baby yarn for fringe: Dark Brown.
Needles: U. S. size 10½-11 / 7 mm: circular.
Notions, optional: decorative button(s).

Instructions

Blue (Red) wrist warmers: CO 25 (15) sts. Working back and forth, knit 35 (17) ridges (1 ridge = 2 rows). BO. Seam cast-on and bind-off ends. Weave in ends neatly on WS.

FINISHING
Fringe: Wrap the yarn evenly around a template for desired length. Cut open wraps at one end. Working with pairs of strands (for baby yarn) or one strand for heavier yarn, attach a fringe between each ridge along wrist warmer edge with a crochet hook.
Sew on buttons or other decorative elements as you like.

HAT "WITH A TWIST"

Here's a hat for anyone afraid of messing up their hair. The hat fits the head loosely and might slouch down towards the back of the neck. It's knitted in a lace stripe pattern that causes the piece to twist around slightly. Top the hat with faux fur pompom attached with a button, if you like.

SKILL LEVEL
Intermediate

FINISHED MEASUREMENTS
Circumference: Approx. 23¾ in / 60 cm.

MATERIALS
Yarn: CYCA #3 (DK, light worsted) Du Store Alpakka Sterk (40% Merino wool, 40% alpaca, 20% nylon, 150 yd/137 m / 50 g).
Yarn Amount and Color:
40-50 g: White.
Substitute Yarn: Yarn recommended for gauge of 22 sts in 4 in / 10 cm.
Needles: U. S. size 7 / 4.5 mm: 16 in / 40 cm circular and set of 5 dpn.
Notions: 1 faux fur pompom with button attachment.

GAUGE
18 sts in pattern = 4 in / 10 cm.
Adjust needle size to obtain correct gauge if necessary.

Instructions

With circular, CO 102 sts. Join, being careful not to twist cast-on row; pm for beginning of rnd. Knit 5 rnds. Now work in lace pattern:
Every rnd: (K4, k2tog, yo) around.
When hat measures 9¾ in / 25 cm long, shape crown:
(K4, k2tog) around.
Knit 2 rnds.
(K3, k2tog) around.
Knit 1 rnd.
(K2, k2tog) around,
Knit 1 rnd.
(K1, k2tog) around.
Knit 1 rnd.
(K2tog) around.
Cut yarn and draw end through rem sts; tighten.

FINISHING
Weave in all ends neatly on WS. Securely attach pompom to top of hat.

YARN INFORMATION

Du Store Alpakka yarns may be purchased (with international shipping charges) from:
Knitting with Attitude
www.knitwithattitude.com

Gjestal Cotton (Bomull) Sport yarn is available from:
Dyed & Gone
dyedandgone.com

Rauma yarns are available from:
The Yarn Guys
www.theyarnguys.com

Sandnes yarns may be purchased (with international shipping charges) from:
Scandinavian Knitting Design
www.scandinavianknittingdesign.com

Some yarns—Søstrene Grene yarns, Viking of Norway yarns, and House of Yarn yarns, in particular—may be difficult to find. A variety of additional and substitute yarns are available from:
Webs – America's Yarn Store
75 Service Center Road
Northampton, MA 01060
800-367-9327
yarn.com

LoveKnitting.com
loveknitting.com/us

If you are unable to obtain any of the yarn used in this book, it can be replaced with a yarn of a similar weight and composition. Please note, however, the finished projects may vary slightly from those shown, depending on the yarn used. Try www.yarnsub.com for suggestions.

For more information on selecting or substituting yarn, contact your local yarn shop or an online store; they are familiar with all types of yarns and would be happy to help you. Additionally, the online knitting community at Ravelry.com has forums where you can post questions about specific yarns. Yarns come and go so quickly these days and there are so many beautiful yarns available.